GENERAL THOMAS JAMES

Reproduced from contemporary portrait by an unknown artist, by courtesy of Mrs. Thomas Higginbotham of Maplewood, Missouri, great-granddaughter of General James.

The Lakeside Classics

THREE YEARS AMONG THE INDIANS AND MEXICANS

By General Thomas James

EDITED BY

MILO MILTON QUAIFE

The Lakeside Press

R. R. DONNELLEY & SONS COMPANY

CHICAGO

Christmas, 1953

PUBLISHERS' PREFACE

THIS fifty-first volume of the Lakeside Classics marks another step in a unique publishing venture. The acceptance by its readers volume by volume of both content and format and the fact that the essential purpose of the series has been maintained are matters in which the Publishers take great pride. From the start it has been the aim to present to the patrons and other friends of the Press a volume of interesting reading which would be the product of fine craftsmanship aided by modern equipment and the use of suitable materials of good quality. While we do not wish to break with this tradition of fifty years but rather keep to general characteristics that will identify future volumes as part of a continuing series, yet we recognize that taste in good bookmaking changes gradually over the years. Just as we did twenty-five years ago with the issue of the first volume of the second series, so in this fifty-first volume we have made further changes that reflect the passing of another twenty-five years.

As recently as 1949 the Lanston Monotype Company made the Bulmer face of type used this year available for setting by machine. This type was designed late in the eighteenth century by the artist, William Martin, who cut single-handedly, all of the punches for it, and it was used with great skill by the London printer, William Bulmer. While Martin in his design preserved the essential feeling of "old face" he tempered it by adopting some of the simplifying characteristics of the "modern face" which had begun to find favor in the latter half of the eighteenth century due to the influence of Baskerville, Bodoni, and other type designers. The black letter text heretofore used in the running head has been dropped and the title page too has been simplified by eliminating the rule border, although the traditional use of the text letter with the imprint has been retained.

Progress in the art of paper making has reached a point where pulp made from wood in place of rags gives such promise of very long life that the use of the former all rag content seems no longer essential to insure permanence. This year the S. D. Warren Company, who have furnished paper for all previous volumes of the Classics, are supplying a paper made with this new pulp and we are confident that with respect to strength, surface, workability and general appearance it will be a worthy successor to the paper heretofore used.

We hope our readers will be pleased with the blue color of the binding cloth. The change is made, not because of any dissatisfaction with the red (and before that the dark green) used on previous volumes, but to set the new series apart from its predecessors. It is gratifying to us that this blue cloth too will be supplied by the Interlaken Mill who have furnished the cloth for all volumes of the Classics.

This year we are presenting a narrative dealing with the development of the West which is more of a collector's rarity than most of the former reprints. The circumstances contributing to this rarity are described by Dr. Quaife in the historical introduction which follows. We were fortunate in locating one of the two then known copies in the hands of our friend, that discriminating collector of Americana, Mr. Everett D. Graff. For the loan of his copy for our purpose we are very grateful.

Thomas James' tale recites the trials and experiences of another of those hardy pioneers whose love of adventure and hope of profit led them into usually hazardous and always exciting adventures. One cannot help admire their sterling characteristics of fortitude and determination to overcome all obstacles, and their ability to bear almost unbelievable hardships. James' repeated disappointments and his failure to win fortune cannot detract from his contribution to the expansion of the frontier.

We express our thanks to Dr. Quaife, the eminent Americana scholar, for continuing to act as editor, as well as to all those who gave him help in his search for material and preparing it for publication.

In entering on this third twenty-five year series of the Lakeside Classics the Publishers can make no promise of continuity of subject matter, either as to time or place. Rather we can say again that we will "attempt to find a historical subject of human interest, which because it has not been previously published or because of its rarity will come fresh to the average reader."

With the hope that the new Lakeside Classics will continue to please the many friends of the Press, we send our best wishes for Christmas and the New Year.

THE PUBLISHERS

Christmas, 1953

CONTENTS

ILLUSTRATIONS

HISTORICAL INTRODUCTION

GENERAL THOMAS JAMES, to whose narrative the present volume of The Lakeside Classics is devoted, pioneered on two widely separated frontiers. As a member of the St. Louis Missouri Fur Company's expedition of 1809–10 to the headwaters of the Missouri he was one of the first Americans to traverse this then remote area; and as a trader to Santa Fe and to the Comanche Indians in the years 1821–23 he was again one of the first Americans to traverse and describe the southwestern area extending from St. Louis to Santa Fe.

The reader of his old-age narrative of his trading experiences, reproduced in the present volume, has an enjoyable treat in store. General James' experiences were frequently thrilling and his recital of them is detailed and vivid. Although his story was first published over a century ago, for reasons which will presently be explained existing copies are exceedingly rare, and even copies of the reprint edition issued in 1916 are difficult to obtain. Although they may be found in numerous reference libraries, it is probably safe to say that but few of our present readers have ever enjoyed the pleasure of reading General James' narrative.

To orient them in its background is my present agreeable task. General Thomas James was born in Maryland, of Welsh parentage, November 4, 1782.[1] Some years later (the date undetermined) his parents, Joseph Austin and Elizabeth (Hosten) James, migrated to Kentucky where James, a younger brother of Thomas, was born in 1798. About the year 1803 the family removed from Kentucky to the American Bottom of southern Illinois.[2]

The American Bottom was the fabulously rich flood plain adjoining the eastern side of the Mississippi for 100 miles from about the vicinity of Alton southward. Here, early in the seventeenth century, adventurous French settlers had founded the settlements of the Illinois country which George Rogers Clark visited and occupied in

---

[1] Details concerning the family history have been derived from General James' own family Bible, now owned by his great-granddaughter, Mrs. Joseph D. Casey of Potosi, Missouri, and from other records in her possession, along with word-of-mouth knowledge handed down from her mother. A genealogical chart prepared by her and by Charles A. James of Amarillo, Texas, a great-grandson of the General, which has been placed at my disposal, supplies detailed data concerning the General's descendants. The birth-date, given on the General's tombstone as November 1, 1782, is recorded in the family Bible as November 4.

[2] The General's old-age narrative says "in the year 1803 when [I was] twenty-two years of age." Obviously there is a slight discrepancy between the date and the age as thus stated.

1778.[3] When, somewhat later, American settlers began to enter Illinois, they located, as a matter of course, among their French predecessors in the American Bottom, where James was to pass most of his remaining life.

In 1807 as he tells us, but more probably in 1806,[4] now a mature man, he accompanied his father on still another migration, this time to the old French-American settlement of Florissant, on the Missouri a short distance above St. Louis. Here Joseph James acquired a strip of land on the Common which now forms a portion of the Seminary farm, and his name, along with those of his sons, Thomas and John G. James, is signed to a record of the parishioners on Feb. 16, 1814 endorsing a new code of parochial regulations.[5] John G. James married Julie Creely, and at his

---

[3] Nominally subject to British rule prior to Clark's advent in their midst, the French cheerfully adhered to the Revolutionary cause and even supplied, in large part, the army which Clark led on his celebrated march to the capture of Lieutenant Governor Hamilton at Vincennes, in February, 1779.

[4] He fixes the date as the year when the Lewis and Clark Expedition returned to St. Louis. This was in 1806.

[5] For data concerning the family at Florissant, see Rev. Gilbert J. Garraghan, *Saint Ferdinand de Florissant* (Chicago, 1923), 61–62. The fact that James, the younger brother, did not sign the document affords a faint clue to the date of the family migration from Maryland to Kentucky. Presumably James was still a minor in 1814, which would suggest that the removal to Kentucky must have occurred in or subsequent to 1794.

death in 1834 left nine living children. One of them, Samuel James, became a judge of the St. Louis County Circuit Court, and lived out his entire life in the house in which he was born, built in 1817 at the corner of St. Louis and St. Peter streets. It was of characteristic French construction, standing amid grounds which comprised the entire square.

From the time of the Spanish regime, St. Louis had been a center of the fur trade, and long in advance of Lewis and Clark enterprising St. Louis merchants had explored far up the Missouri and dreamed of opening an overland highway to the Pacific. Under American rule and a new government that highway had now been found, and the information which Lewis and Clark brought back to St. Louis filled many frontiersmen with the ambition to exploit the riches in furs whose existence the explorers had revealed.

Aside from a few lone individuals, the foremost to embark in the new field of endeavor were the group of St. Louis merchants and officials who in the spring of 1809 associated themselves together as partners in the St. Louis Missouri Fur Company. Their immediate incitement to this action proceeded from one of the consequences of the Lewis and Clark expedition, which had been accompanied on its return to St. Louis in 1806 by the friendly Mandan chief, Shehaka. He had been conducted upon a tour to Washington to visit the Great White Father, after which, in the summer of 1807, a government expedition led by Nathaniel Pryor, one of Lewis and Clark's trusted subordinates, had undertaken to escort him in safety to his North Dakota home. It had been attacked by the Arikaras, however, and compelled to return to St. Louis with the unfortunate chieftain. Now a more determined attempt to escort him to his anxious subjects was about to be made by the Government.

The founders of the Missouri Fur Company now entered into a contract with the Government to escort Shehaka to his Mandan home. To accomplish this, a formidable force of riflemen and voyageurs, the former enrolled as a detachment of Missouri Territorial Militia, was organized under the command of Colonel Pierre Chouteau. Upon the delivery of Shehaka to his followers the expedition was to become transformed into a private trading organization under the leadership of Manuel Lisa for the prosecution of the fur trade on the headwaters of the Missouri.

Thomas James, already a seasoned frontiersman, enlisted as a rifleman for the expedition, and to the relation of his exciting and financially disastrous experiences the first two chapters of his book are devoted. When the military aspect of the expedition had been accomplished James was to continue as the leader of a small band of trappers whose equipment and compensation were provided for in a contract which was entered upon at St. Louis at the time of his enlistment.

The contract, signed on March 29, 1809, provided for three years of employment by James, during which he was to perform such services as might be required of him by the agents of the Company. Details aside, he was to "do and perform all these things which men engaged under similar circumstances and with the same views are bound to do and perform, obeying and executing with promptness all lawful and reasonable orders" which might be given him by his employers.

Seldom if ever has a more unhappy contract been made than the one between the Fur Company and the men (of whom James was but one) who were to conduct its trapping operations. The expedition had hardly started on its up-river voyage when discord and insubordination among its members became rampant. To the student of the American fur trade the reasons for this development are sufficiently obvious. The fur trade was a specialized calling whose methods of work and standards of employment had become fixed by two hundred years of practice. Indispensable to its prosecution were the Canadian voyageurs, whose patient endurance of hardship and sub-

mission to their employers finds but few counter-
parts in recorded history.

These men comprised one important half of the
expedition. At the opposite pole from them in
character and temperament was the group of
Americans to which James belonged. Individually
brave and pugnacious, they had no more conception of submission to their superiors than the wild
animals of the western Plains. Quickly tiring of
the scanty fare and monotonous toil which the
voyageurs accepted as a matter of course, they
resorted to riotous conduct, indulging in wild
threats against their employers and defying every
effort of the latter to enforce a state of discipline.

Such conduct could not fail to have its effect
upon the partners of the Company, as even James
recognized, despite his subsequent hostility toward them. To what extent the misconduct of the
Americans justified the refusal of the partners to
fulfill the obligations they had assumed, we do not
attempt to determine. The reader will see for himself how bitterly James accused them of wholesale
dishonesty. Since they numbered many of the
foremost merchants of St. Louis, his accusations
were but little heeded in that community and even
as recently as 1916 the official of the Missouri
Historical Society seriously debated the propriety
of reprinting his narrative. For the present publishers and Editor no such scruple exists. The

American fur trade of a century and a half ago was a hard-bitten calling, whose leaders enjoyed no monopoly of honesty and fairness. James is entitled to a hearing no less than any other American, and his charges against the Company to such credit as they may seem to the reader to deserve.

Back in St. Louis in 1810, penniless and beset by law-suits, James went back to Pennsylvania where he found himself a bride. Two years were devoted to this sojourn, when he returned to the West and from 1813 to 1815 engaged in transporting goods by keel boat between Pittsburgh and St. Louis. Although this calling was both laborious and hazardous, the profits he reaped from it were large.

Why he abandoned it is not recorded, but in 1815 he returned to the American Bottom to enter upon a mercantile career. Harrisonville in Monroe County, the scene of his operations, was only a hamlet, but it was a shipping point for the interior country and directly opposite the Missouri town of Herculaneum, the entrepot of the lead mines of eastern Missouri.

Save for occasional absences, James passed the remainder of his life at Harrisonville and (subsequently) at near-by Monroe City. Old Harrisonville, where he began his mercantile career, was gradually washed away by the Mississippi River, and about the year 1840 the site was abandoned in favor of a new one a short distance inland. Although in 1844 even this location was flooded twelve feet deep, a third of a century later it was still occupied, having several businesses and a corresponding number of families. Today it is a hamlet of about a dozen houses and a single general country store.

The town site of old Harrisonville, originally known as Carthage, was sold by John Edgar, a well-known resident of Kaskaskia, to John Mc-Knight and Thomas Brady of St. Louis. They acquired extensive landholdings in St. Louis and elsewhere, among them being the Harrisonville property, of which James became the manager. The Monroe County historian states that Frederick Dent of St. Louis, the future father-in-law of General U. S. Grant, owned an interest in the store, to which he was a frequent visitor.

Eventually James opened a store in New Harrisonville, from which he subsequently removed several miles farther inland to the farm of Andrew Kinney, at the edge of the bluff which hems the Mississippi bottom. Here a gulch, traversed by a small stream which comes down from the higher land to the flood plain, breaks the continuity of the bluff. Half a mile or more up the gulch a superb spring of living water issues from the rocky side-wall to feed the little stream. Some rods below it a dam, whose remains may still be seen, was built across the stream and the head of water thus obtained was conducted to the mill, which was erected at a widening of the gulch some rods still farther down.

Here Joseph Kinney had settled in 1793 and Andrew, one of his many sons, had subsequently built the water mill, which was known by his name. The date when James acquired it is unknown, but it must have been soon after his return from his final trading expedition in 1823. At any rate, he was appointed postmaster in 1827, at which time and until his death twenty years later the place was known as James' Mill. How, or when, it acquired its present name of Monroe City has not been learned. It now (1953) comprises a dozen or more houses strung along the sides of the gulch, to which the name of "City" seems oddly inappropriate.[6]

Despite a crushing burden of debt, incurred in consequence of his trading expeditions to Santa Fe and to the Comanches in 1821–23, James retained the confidence and respect of his neighbors. In 1825 they elected him to the State Legislature, and in the same year he was elected General of the Second Brigade, First Division of

[6] On the map of Illinois published at Boston in 1850 and reproduced in Vol. I of the Lakeside Classics edition of Governor Thomas Ford's *History of Illinois*, published in 1945, it was still shown as "James' Mill Postoffice."

Illinois Militia. Both this office and the postmastership were still retained by him in 1846, when his narrative was published. Since he died the following year, it seems certain he retained them until the close of his life.

Two extensive absences from home, both related in this book, interrupted his long mercantile career. In 1818, as he tells us, an inopportune deficiency of water in the Ohio River so delayed the shipment of a stock of goods he had purchased in Baltimore that he was reduced to a state of impending bankruptcy. In an effort to retrieve his fortune he embarked with John McKnight upon the trading expedition to Santa Fe which is related in Chapters III to VI of his narrative. From it posterity gained another thrilling story, but the narrator reaped only fresh disaster and a new burden of debt.

Faced anew with financial ruin, James made still another effort to retrieve his fortune. In the winter of 1822–23, again in association with John McKnight, he launched the trading adventure to the Comanches whose story he relates in the two concluding chapters of his narrative: McKnight lost his life and James lost the property he had risked—obtained on credit at St. Louis, probably on the strength of McKnight's financial standing.

Bereft of fortune but not of honor, James now resigned himself to a life of poverty and humdrum toil in the effort to rear his family and discharge his mountainous burden of debt. Both objectives were finally achieved. Twenty years of effort, facilitated by the support of a considerate and helpful brother, enabled him to discharge his debts and to bequeath to his children "a good example and an unsullied name." At the end, advanced in years and broken in health, he harbored no bitterness for his lot, rejoicing, instead, in the numerous manifestations of respect conferred upon him by his fellow citizens. Proof of his indomitable spirit is seen in his statement almost at the close of his life that but for his advanced age he would embark anew upon the Indian trade, despite the disasters he had formerly encountered.

An aspect of James' career which finds no mention in his narrative deserves inclusion here. In addition to his milling activities, for a quarter of a century or more he practiced medicine in Monroe County. How or when he learned this art we have no record. Perhaps, like Rebecca Burlend, whose narrative of life in pioneer Illinois, *A True Picture of Emigration*, was published as the Lakeside Classics volume for 1936, he acquired it by the process of exercising a native aptitude. Prolonged training in the acquirement of special skills was an unknown thing on the American frontier, and one might practice medicine or anything else for which he could obtain the approval of his associates.

James imparted his medical lore to his son, Lewis, born in 1819, who continued to practice at Monroe City until about the year 1868, when he removed to Jefferson County, Missouri. Eventually he settled at near-by Racola, Washington County, where he continued in practice until within a few years of his death at an advanced age in January, 1904.[7] Interesting evidence concerning medical conditions in Missouri a century ago is afforded by his admission—already a veteran practitioner—to the St. Louis Medical College in October, 1858, from which he was graduated in March, 1859, although he was not licensed by the State Board until 1883.

Necessarily, having in view the circumstances surrounding his life, General James' formal schooling must have been meager.[8] The literary excellence of his narrative, however, betrays no hint of this, compelling the inference that he must

[7]Although his published obituary gives his age at death (January 16, 1904) as "84 years 2 months and 5 days," Dr. James himself stated (in letter to Frank E. Stevens, Oct. 21, 1902) that he would be eighty-three on the coming Nov. 11, thus fixing his birthdate as Nov. 11, 1819. In a letter to Stevens on Jan. 22, 1903 he stated that his father had practiced medicine thirty years in Monroe County. Mrs. Casey of Potosi has her grandfather's record book of medical practice at Monroe City from 1849 to 1868, and his diploma from the St. Louis Medical College in March, 1859.

[8]The letters written by his son, Dr. Lewis James, to Frank E. Stevens in 1902 and 1903 disclose, in like fashion, his own meager schooling.

have enjoyed the assistance of a collaborator in composing it. This consideration led Judge Douglas, who edited the reprint edition published by the Missouri Historical Society in 1916, to inquire of Dr. John F. Snyder, veteran historian of southern Illinois, what he might know about the matter.[9]

In response, Dr. Snyder related that Nathaniel Niles, a lawyer and resident of Belleville, had written the narrative at General James' dictation. Niles was born at Plainfield, New York, in 1817. He studied law in New York City and about the year 1840 migrated to Belleville, where he taught school (Snyder was one of his pupils), practiced law and politics, and as other side lines edited a newspaper and served in the Mexican and the Civil War. He was a devotee of literature, whose years of retirement were chiefly passed in the Belleville Library.[10] He was thus well equipped

[9]Dr. Snyder died in 1921 in his ninety-first year. To his industry in unraveling the puzzle, we owe our knowledge of the terrible fate which overtook the sons of Governor Thomas Ford. See first volume of the Lakeside Classics edition of his *History of Illinois*, published in 1945, pp. XXIX–XXXIII.

[10]Although Niles was a prominent citizen, the facts concerning his career have been assembled only with difficulty. He enlisted for the Mexican War with the rank of lieutenant in the Second Illinois Regiment in June, 1846, and was absent from Illinois until late midsummer of 1847. His card in the Belleville *Advocate* announcing his

to ghost write General James' narrative, and we can only regret that Dr. Snyder's statements concerning his agency omit much we would like to know.

General James was a man of positive temper and his narrative does not spare the many persons who incurred his dislike. Among these were the missionaries whom he encountered and the partners of the St. Louis Missouri Fur Company in whose employ he engaged for the expedition of 1809–10 to the Upper Missouri. "The book had barely been issued from the press," wrote Snyder to Judge Douglas, "when it was severely attacked by several newspapers—and I think the old *Missouri Republican* was one of them. Niles immediately suppressed it, gathered all the copies he could secure and destroyed them. For a long time it was a delicate subject to mention to him, but in later years when it *was* mentioned, he did

resumption of legal practice is dated September 23, 1847. He subsequently served one or more terms in the State Legislature and for several terms (until 1861) as county judge. For several years, during the fifties, he also owned and edited the Belleville *Advocate*, which was the recognized organ of the Republican Party in St. Clair County. During much of the Civil War he was Colonel of the 130th Illinois Regiment, which was mustered Oct. 25, 1862. A letter denying the report that he had ghosted Governor John Reynolds' books is in the Ill. State Hist. Soc. *Journal*, IV, 92–94. He died in his eighty-fourth year, Sept. 16, 1900.

not swear so much but regarded it as a good joke."[11]

Thus the subsequent rarity of the original edition is explained, at least in part. Presumably the attacks which induced its attempted suppression emanated from the founders and friends of the St. Louis Missouri Fur Company partners. But it is impossible to believe that General James, who lived until December, 1847, had any part in the suppression, and Dr. Snyder's story affords no explanation of what right Niles had to perpetrate it. The book itself contains no hint of his agency in producing it, nor any indication that any one other than General James was responsible for it. Unless Colonel Niles financed its publication, it is not apparent why he should have manifested such an active concern over its hostile reception.

Dr. Snyder states that the attacks upon the book began at once following its publication and that Niles "immediately" suppressed the edition. Since he was absent from the state from June, 1846 to about September, 1847, this implies that the suppression must have been undertaken prior to his departure. We do not know in what month in 1846 the book was published, but the foregoing would indicate that it must have been consider-

[11]Judge Douglas' Introduction to the Missouri Historical Society edition of James' narrative, p. 8. This edition will be cited henceforth simply as "Douglas."

ably prior to June, for the hostile criticisms to have been published and Niles' destruction of the edition to have been accomplished. Examination of the file of the *Missouri Republican*, preserved in the Missouri Historical Society Library, from July, 1846 to July, 1847, and of the Belleville *Advocate* file, preserved in the Belleville Public Library, for a somewhat longer period, disclosed no mention of James' book.

Dr. Snyder was a boy in 1846, and an octogenarian in 1916. Our general knowledge of the fallibility of old-age memories apart, his short statement to Judge Douglas contains several obvious errors. Yet he was a much more competent witness than the average one, and there seems no reason to question his ascription of the literary composition of James' narrative to Colonel Niles. Why the latter, a lawyer and a disinterested person, did not foresee the attacks which the bitterness of General James' recital was bound to provoke, and exert his personal influence and literary skill to temper them, one can only wonder.

The book was printed in a small-town frontier newspaper office. Because of General James' unfortunate loss of his journals, it is an old-age narrative of memories which he had often related to his friends before he undertook to secure their publication. Although he possessed a keen memory, it was inevitable that with the passage of years and with repeated retellings his recollection of events would undergo a certain amount of change. That he was a man of strong feelings is evident. That these operated to intensify his disparagement of those who ill-treated him, or with whom he quarreled, is a reasonable presumption.

This, of course, is regrettable, but whatever his faults may have been he was a sturdy and patriotic American. He dared the rigors of the northern winters and the hardships of the southwestern deserts. Dangers from the savages and from the wilderness apart, the mere physical toil which his expeditions involved is appalling to contemplate. He was one among uncounted path breakers who dared their lives in the effort to redeem America from its former savage to its present civilized state. He left to his children "a good example and an unsullied name." He toiled for a quarter of a century to discharge his debts, and succeeded in doing so. He died intestate on December 17, 1847, and a few weeks later his brother obtained letters of administration upon his estate, for which he gave bond in the sum of $200. Unfortunately the itemized report which he was required to make to the court can no longer be found among the county records.[12]

[12]General James and his wife, Catherine, are buried in the old Catholic cemetery at Madonnaville, a short distance from Monroe City, where their graves and head-

Varying reports have been given of General James' personal appearance. Dr. Snyder, who in boyhood saw him several times, seventy years later described him as "an ordinary looking man, six feet tall, muscular, and of the coon-hunter type."[13] W. J. Ghent, his biographer in the *Dictionary of American Biography*, however, declares that "his portrait in the Douglas volume reveals . . . intelligence, will, and candor, and refutes [the] unfriendly characterization of him" by Dr. Snyder which has just been cited. The Douglas portrait, however, was "redrawn" from the photograph of the original published by Stevens in his *Black Hawk War*. Concerning it, Stevens' St. Louis agent wrote in 1902: "He [the photographer] could not bring out the yellow buttons and epaulettes at all. The face (as you see) is a regular Andrew Jackson and he looks every inch a *warrior* in the portrait, but the dark background and the dark blue military coat would not take."

stones may still be seen. Regrettably, I did not learn of this when I visited Monroe City. Mrs. Joseph D. Casey, great-granddaughter of General James, who visited the cemetery in April, 1953 informs me (letter of April 5) that Madonnaville, although a very old settlement, is still a tiny one, consisting mainly of a rock church, rock school, and rock rectory, all made of native stone and quite nice. The inscription on General James' headstone is considerably eroded.

[13]Douglas, 8.

In 1916, when Judge Douglas edited the Missouri Historical Society edition of James' narrative, he could learn of but two existing copies of the book; one, the copy owned by the Society, the other a copy which had been sold in Philadelphia in 1912, whose current possessor was unknown. Several additional copies have since come to light, one of them in the library of St. Louis University. According to a contemporary newspaper report it was sold by the University for $950 and immediately resold for $1150. Copies of the 1916 edition, which numbered but 365, are relatively scarce, and command a price, when available, of $50 or more.

In editing the present edition I have utilized a photostat copy of one of the rare original volumes which the owner, Mr. Everett D. Graff of Winnetka, Illinois has made available to the publishers. I have also levied freely upon the extensive editorial data included in the 1916 edition by Judge Douglas. In view of the circumstances, recited above, attending the production of the book, I have deemed it undesirable to reproduce *literatim* the inadvertent errors and other crudities of the original edition. Instead, I have eliminated these whenever such procedure has seemed to me to be desirable, and have substituted new chapter heads for the résumé of chapter contents in the original edition. In short, I have endeavored to

present General James' narrative to the reader in
an acceptable form as he himself would have desired to achieve. The present introduction, along
with the illustrations, footnotes, and index formed
no part, of course, of the original edition.

Many individuals, some of them total strangers
to me, have contributed more or less importantly
to the performance of my editorial task. From
Mrs. Elleine Stones and her staff of workers in
the Burton Historical Collection of the Detroit
Public Library I have received unfailing courtesies
and assistance. The Librarian of the Belleville
Public Library and Director Charles Van Ravens-
waay of the Missouri Historical Society accorded
access to the files of early Belleville and St. Louis
newspapers in their custody. Mrs. Joseph D.
Casey of Potosi, Mo., great-granddaughter of
General James, responded generously to my ap-
peal for family data and records in her possession.
Her sister, Mrs. Thomas Higginbotham of Maplewood, Mo., granted permission to photograph
the portrait of General James, now in her possession. Mr. Charles A. James of Amarillo, Texas, a
great-grandson, supplied a genealogical chart of
the family, compiled by himself and Mrs. Joseph
D. Casey. Mr. and Mrs. William B. Huckabay
of Monroe City, Illinois supplied local guidance
and helpful information upon my visit to that
place.[14] Mr. Gordon Hicks of Sycamore, Illinois

and his daughter Sarah of Chicago exerted themselves to find and send me the correspondence
had by Frank E. Stevens in 1902 over the pro-
cural of the copy of General James' portrait which
he reproduced in his *Black Hawk War.* "We were
glad to help you," wrote Miss Hicks, "as I am
sure my grandfather had to use this same method
to obtain many of his pictures for the *Black Hawk*
book." Mr. Eugene C. Ferris of Clarksville,
Arkansas and Mr. Horace Hutson of Spadra
supplied local information concerning the grave
of Matthew Lyon. Mrs. Lucille R. Wyant drew
for me the two maps which accompany General
James' narrative of his trading activities. Finally,
the publishers made possible my visit to the scenes
of the narrative and my wife, Letitia, in addition
to performing my secretarial work chauffeured
me on the 2800-mile journey. To all of these,
along with numerous others who aided me in
various ways, my sincere appreciation is tendered.

M. M. QUAIFE.

[14]They believe the residence they occupy, which stands
a short distance from the ruins of the mill, was formerly
the home of General James.

THREE YEARS AMONG

THE

INDIANS AND MEXICANS.

BY GEN. THOMAS JAMES,
OF MONROE COUNTY, ILLINOIS.

WATERLOO, ILL.
PRINTED AT THE OFFICE OF THE "WAR EAGLE."
1846.

Three Years
Among the Indians
and Mexicans

Three Years
Among the Indians
and Mexicans

CHAPTER I

From St. Louis to the Three Forks

I HAVE often amused myself and friends by relating stories of my adventures in the West, and am led to believe by the, perhaps, too partial representations of those friends that my life in the prairies and mountains for three years is worthy of a record more enduring than their memories. I have passed a year and a half on the headwaters of the Missouri and among the gorges of the Rocky Mountains as a hunter and a trapper and two years among the Spaniards and Comanches. I have suffered much from the inclemency of nature and of man, had many "hair breadth 'scapes," and acquired considerable information illustrative of Indian and Mexican character and customs. By a plain, unvarnished tale of western life, of perils and of hardships, I hope to amuse the reader who delights in accounts of wild adventure, though found out of the pages of a novel and possessing no attraction but their unadorned truthfulness. I am now on the shady side of sixty, with mind and memory unimpaired. If my reminiscences, as recorded in the following pages, serve to awaken my countrymen of the West and Southwest, now, thank God, including Texas, to the importance of peaceful and friendly relations with the most powerful tribe of Indians on the continent, the Comanches, I shall not regard the labor of preparing these sheets as bestowed in vain.[1]

[1] The Comanche tribe was an offshoot from the Shoshone of Wyoming, which was driven southward by the pressure of the Sioux into the southern Great Plains area. They were nomads whose chief economic dependence was upon the buffaloes. By the Medicine Lodge Treaty of 1867 they agreed to settle upon a reservation between the Washita and the Red River in southwestern Oklahoma, but not until they were finally subdued several years later, as recorded in General Custer's *My Life on the Plains* (the Lakeside Classics volume for 1952) did they finally do so. Prior to this forced settlement, they ranged widely, from the Platte River on the north to Durango in Mexico on the south. The Comanches were never as powerful as the author's statement suggests. But they were superb horsemen and until their final subjection there could be no settlement of the southern plains. In 1904 they numbered about 1400, attached to the Kiowa Agency in Oklahoma. F. W. Hodge, *Handbook of American Indians north of Mexico.*

Texas was admitted to the Union, Dec. 29, 1845. Unless this statement is the product of subsequent revision of the manuscript, it indicates that it must have been wholly written in the year 1846.

In the year 1803, when twenty-two years of age, I emigrated with my father from Kentucky to Illinois. In the spring of 1807 we removed from Illinois to Missouri, which were then both Territories, and settled in the town of St. Ferdinand, near St. Louis.[2] In the fall of this year Lewis and Clark returned from Oregon and the Pacific Ocean, whither they had been sent by the administration of Jefferson in the first exploring expedition west of the Rocky Mountains, and their accounts of that wild region, with those of their companions, first excited a spirit of trafficking adventure among the young men of the West.[3] They had brought with them from

[2]St. Ferdinand, more commonly known as Florissant, is in St. Louis County, about 17 miles northward of St. Louis. It was founded during the American Revolution and by the close of the century had become a settlement of about 60 houses. Many of the residents engaged in the western fur trade as associates of the "Mountain Men" of the early nineteenth century. Illustrative of the Arcadian simplicity of life at the beginning of the century is the story that the first lock placed on a smoke-house door by a resident created general indignation. In 1950 the town had a population of about 3700; for details concerning its history see Rev. Gilbert J. Garraghan, *Saint Ferdinand de Florissant.*

[3]Lewis and Clark returned from their transcontinental exploration in 1806. Although James evidently possessed an uncommonly good memory, occasional slips in his old-age narrative sometimes occur. The first attempt to return Shehaka to his tribe was made in 1807 instead of 1808.

the Upper Missouri a chief named Shehaka, of
the Mandan tribe of Indians.[4] This chief, in
company with Lewis and Clark, visited the
"Great Father" at Washington City and returned to St. Louis in the following spring (1807)
with Lewis, who, in the mean time had been appointed Governor of Missouri Territory. He sent
the Chief Shehaka up the Missouri with an escort
of about forty United States troops, under Capt.
Pryor.[5] On their arrival in the country of the

[4]Shehaka, or Big White, was principal chief of the
lower Mandan village at the time of Lewis and Clark's
winter sojourn of 1804–1805. On November 12 he paid a
friendly visit to the explorers' winter camp, accompanied
by his squaw who, in addition to his child, "pack'd about
100 lb of fine meet" as a present for the white men. Upon
the explorers' return from the Pacific in 1806 Shehaka
and his squaw accompanied them to St. Louis in order to
pay a visit to the President at Washington. The difficulty
attending their return is related by our author. After all
his troubles, Shehaka encountered a sad fate. His extrava-
gant tales of the wonders he had seen were treated with
contempt by his fellow tribesmen, since the Mandans, as
the traveler Brackenridge reports, "treat with ridicule
the idea of there being a greater or more numerous people
than themselves." Moreover, he had not won distinction
as a warrior, the one sure pathway to fame among the
American Indians. In 1812 Shehaka paid another visit to
St. Louis, accompanied by his wife and several warriors.
He was killed by a party of Gros Ventres (Minitaree),
apparently while returning from this visit.

[5]Nathaniel Pryor of Kentucky was one of the four ser-
geants of the Lewis and Clark expedition. He was a capable man of excellent character, whose career was studded
with mishaps and disappointments. On February 27,

Arikaras,[6] a warlike tribe next east or this side of the Mandans, they were attacked by the former tribe, and eight or ten soldiers killed.

1807 he enlisted in the regular army with the rank of ensign, serving until April 1, 1810. He then established a trading post near Galena, Illinois, which was sacked by a party of Winnebagoes at the opening of the War of 1812, Pryor escaping with his life but with the loss of all his property. He subsequently rejoined the army, becoming a captain on October 1, 1814. He served under Jackson at New Orleans, and according to General Sam Houston "a braver man never fought under your [Jackson's] eagles." Following the close of the war he again engaged in the Indian trade, married an Osage woman, and from 1820 on lived with that tribe. He died June 10, 1831. His grave, unmarked save for a marker erected nearby by Mr. Thomas J. Harrison of Pryor, occupies a secluded spot overlooking Pryor Creek, about five miles southeast of Pryor, Oklahoma.

[6]The Arikaras comprised the northerly division of the Caddoan family, which was scattered throughout the Plains region from Texas northward. They eventually became allied with the Mandans and the Hidatsa of Dakota. They were disposed to be friendly to the whites when Lewis and Clark encountered them in 1804–1805. They subsequently had many disputes with the early traders, following the repulse of Nathaniel Pryor's expedition of 1807. In 1823 they attacked the William H. Ashley party, driving it back and killing a number of its members. Colonel Henry Leavenworth, then in command of Fort Atkinson near Omaha, led an expedition to punish them, which was attended with but dubious results. However, the Arikaras abandoned their villages near the mouth of Grand River, eventually removing to the vicinity of the Mandans at Fort Berthold, where General De Trobriand encountered them in the later sixties. See his *Army Life in Dakota*, the Lakeside Classics volume for 1941.

This event so disheartened the rest that they returned with Shehaka to St. Louis.

The Missouri Fur Company had just been formed and they projected an expedition up the Missouri and to the Rocky Mountains, which was to start in the spring of the following year, 1809.[7] The company consisted of ten partners, among whom was M. Gratiot, Pierre Menard, Sam'l. Morrison, Pierre Chouteau, Manuel Lisa, Major Henry, M. Labbadie, and Reuben Lewis. Gov. Lewis was also said to have had an interest in the concern. The company contracted with him to convey the Mandan chief to his tribe for the sum, as I was informed, of $10,000.[8] I en-

[7] This was the St. Louis Missouri Fur Company, whose activities from 1809 to 1811 should not be confused with later companies having similar names. In the 1916 edition of James' narrative, edited by Walter B. Douglas, the articles of association of the Company are printed (pp. 250–55).

[8] The contract, dated Feb. 24, 1809, is printed by Douglas, 267–70. It required the Fur Company to raise an armed force of 125 men, under the command of Pierre Chouteau, which should conduct Shehaka and his family in safety to the Mandan towns. Until his arrival there, the force was to constitute a body of the Missouri Territorial Militia. Besides Shehaka's family, the family of René Jessaume, a French Canadian who had served Lewis and Clark in the capacity of interpreter and who had accompanied Shehaka to Washington in the same capacity, was to be conveyed to the Mandan towns. In return for the faithful performance of its obligations the Company was to be paid $7000, and the Governor further

listed in this expedition, which was raised for trading with the Indians and trapping for beaver on the headwaters of the Missouri and Columbia rivers.

The whole party, at starting, consisted of 350 men, of whom about one-half were Americans and the remainder Canadian Frenchmen and Creoles of Kaskaskia, St. Louis, and other places. The French were all veteran *voyageurs*, thoroughly inured to boating and trapping. Manuel Lisa, called by the men "Esaw", had enlisted many of them in Detroit for this expedition, and hired them by the year. We Americans were all private adventurers, each on his own hook, and were led into the enterprise by the promises of the Company, who agreed to subsist us to the trapping grounds, we helping to navigate the boats, and on our arrival there they were to furnish us each with a rifle and sufficient ammunition, six good beaver traps, and also four men of their hired French, to be under our individual commands for a period of three years.[9]

agreed that no other person would be authorized by him to ascend the Missouri above the mouth of the Platte prior to the last day fixed for the departure of the expedition.

Chouteau's report upon his successful conduct of the expedition is also printed by Douglas, 273–78.

[9]The primary purpose of the Company was to prosecute the fur trade; the delivery of Shehaka to his home was an incidental objective. The contract of the Company with the Government required it to raise a force of 125 men,

By the terms of the contract each of us was to divide one-fourth of the profits of our joint labor with the four men thus to be appointed to us. How we were deceived and taken in will be seen in the sequel. The Company made us the fairest promises in St. Louis, only to break them in the Indian country. Lisa, or Esaw, or Manuel as he was variously called, had the principal command.[10] He was a Spaniard or Mexican by birth, and bore a very bad reputation in the country and among the Americans. He had

40 of whom should be Americans and "expert riflemen." To this contingent, James, of course, belonged. The French-Canadian voyageurs were expert canoe men, accustomed to extraordinary labor and scanty fare, who for generations had constituted the backbone of the fur trade. There is no reason to suppose that Lisa and Chouteau, on this expedition, treated them in other than the customary manner. To the American contingent, however, proud frontiersmen and without experience in the fur trade, such treatment was intolerable, as James' narrative sufficiently shows. The great hiving ground of the *voyageurs* was French Quebec. By 1800, however, such western places as Detroit and Mackinac had become lesser centers of supply. James' contract with the Fur Company is printed by Douglas, pp. 271–72.

[10]The commander of the military expedition was Chouteau. Upon the delivery of Shehaka, the party was to assume its fur-trading character, under the leadership of Lisa. Lisa was born at New Orleans, of Spanish parentage, Sept. 8, 1772. In early manhood he migrated to St. Louis, which remained his home until his death, August 12, 1820. A controversial character, he was praised by some contemporaries and derided by many. He acquired

been on the head-waters of the Missouri the year before with a company of about fifty men and had met with great success in catching beaver and trading with the Indians. He had built a fort, called Manuel's fort at the junction or fork of the Big Horn and Yellowstone rivers, and left a garrison of hunters in it when he returned in the spring of this year and went into the Missouri Fur Company. He was suspected of having invited the Arikaras to attack the Government troops under Capt. Pryor, with Shehaka the year before,[11] for the purpose of preventing the traders and trappers who were with the troops from getting into the Upper Country. Mr. Chouteau and Col. Menard acted jointly with Lisa in conducting the expedition. I went as steersman or captain of one of the barges, with about twenty-four men, all Americans, under my command. There were thirteen barges and keel

great influence over the Indians, which he explained by saying that he treated them fairly instead of robbing them. In 1807 he led an expedition to the Upper Missouri which established a post, subsequently known as Fort Manuel, on the Yellowstone at the mouth of the Big Horn River. A man of great energy, he was perhaps the foremost pioneer in the fur trade of the Upper Missouri. Between 1807 and his death in 1820 he is said to have traveled 26,000 miles by boat in the course of his numerous up-river voyages.

[11]More correctly, two years before. James is here following his earlier error in stating that Captain Pryor's expedition occurred in 1808, instead of 1807.

boats in all. On my barge I had Doctor Thomas, the surgeon of the company, and Reuben Lewis, brother of Meriwether Lewis, the Governor.

We started from St. Louis in the month of June, 1809, and ascended the Missouri by rowing, pushing with poles, cordeling, or pulling with ropes, warping, and sailing. My crew were light-hearted, jovial men, with no care or anxiety for the future and little fear of any danger. In the morning we regularly started by daybreak and stopped, generally, late at night. The partners, or *bourgeoises,* as the French called them, were in the forward barge, with a strong crew of hardy and skilful *voyageurs,* and there Lisa and some of his colleagues lorded it over the poor fellows most arrogantly, and made them work as if their lives depended on their getting forward with the greatest possible speed. They peremptorily required all the boats to stop in company for the night, and our barge being large and heavily loaded, the crew frequently had great difficulty in overtaking them in the evening. We occasionally had races with some of the forward barges, in which my crew of Americans proved themselves equal in a short race to their more experienced French competitors.

We thus continued, with nothing of interest occurring, till we passed the Platte. Six weeks of hard labor on our part had been spent when our

General James' Upper Missouri River Expedition of 1809-10
Route ·········

0   50   100   150   200

N
W — E
S

MONTANA
Helena○
Great Falls○
Missouri River
Three Forks
Fort Henry's Fork
Snake River
IDAHO
Livingston○
Bozeman○
Gallatin R.
Madison River
Jefferson River
Clark Fork River
Yellowstone River
Miles City○
○Fort Manuel
Powder River
Big Horn River
WYOMING
Cheyenne○
North Platte River
South Platte River
UTAH
COLORADO
River
NORTH DAKOTA
Little Missouri
Knife R.
Fort Lisa
Mandan Town
Fort Clark
Bismarck○
Cheyenne River
SOUTH DAKOTA
Pierre○
Rapid City○
Missouri River
James River
Fargo○
Big Sioux River
Sioux Falls○
Sioux City○
Omaha○
○Lincoln
NEBRASKA
Platte River
Blue River
Big Kansas River
River
KANSAS
○Des Moines
MISSOURI
Fort Osage
Kansas City
IOWA
MINNESOTA
Minneapolis○St. Paul
Des Moines River
Mississippi River
WISCONSIN
Duluth○
Lake Superior
ILLINOIS
Illinois River

allotted provisions gave out and we were compelled to live on boiled corn, without salt. At the same time all the other boats were well supplied and the gentlemen proprietors in the leading barge were faring in the most sumptuous and luxurious manner. The French hands were much better treated on all occasions than the Americans. The former were employed for a long period at stated wages and were accustomed to such service and such men as those in command of them, while we were private adventurers for our own benefit, as well as that of the Company, who regarded us with suspicion and distrust. Many Americans on the passage up the river, disgusted with the treatment they received, fell off in small companies and went back. At Coté Sans Dessein, opposite the mouth of the Osage, most of them returned.[12] On reaching the Mandan country we numbered about ten Americans, having

[12]Coté Sans Dessein received its name from a detached limestone hill on the river bank at this point. Henry M. Brackenridge in 1811 reported that the settlement contained 13 French and 2 or 3 Indian families. In 1950 Coté Sans Dessein Township had a population of 600, the village being no longer separately listed in the U.S. census. Here, as earlier, James' statements concerning numbers in the party are inaccurate. Instead of 350 at the start, the actual number was barely half so large. Douglas, p. 272, supplies a list of 31 deserters and of 12 men discharged for disability or incompetence. Many of them had been given advances by the Company, totaling about $3700. Some of them stole the canoe which Lisa

started from St. Louis with about one hundred and seventy-five and an equal number of French.

After passing the Platte River my crew were worn down with hard labor and bad fare. Their boiled corn, without salt or meat, did not sustain them under the fatigue of navigating the barge, and the contrast between their treatment and that of the French enraged them. A meeting was the result. The Company had on our barge thirty barrels of pork, and one morning my crew came to me in a body demanding some of these provisions. I commanded them not to break into the pork without permission, and promised, if they would work and keep up till noon, to procure some for dinner.

At noon, when we stopped, the men rolled up a barrel of pork onto the deck and one of them, named Cheek, bestrided it with a tomahawk, crying out: "Give the word, Captain." I forbade them, as before, and went ashore to find Lewis, who had left the boat at the begining of trouble.[13] He said the pork was the Company's and

stated was taken along for the purpose of procuring provisions for the men. It is evident that insubordination was rampant among the American contingent of the expedition.

[13]This was Reuben Lewis, brother of Governor Meriwether Lewis and a member of the Fur Company. He remained on the Upper Missouri in command of one of the fur trade posts until 1812. Upon his return to St. Louis he was appointed Indian agent to the Quapaws and the

told me not to touch it. I said the men would and should have some of it, and went back to the boat to give the "word" to Cheek. Lewis hastened to the *bourgeoises* in their barge close by, to give the alarm. I could see them in their cabin, from the shore where I stood, playing cards and drinking. Lewis entered with the news that "James' crew were taking the provisions." Manuel Lisa seized his pistols and ran out, followed by the other partners. "What the devil," said he to me, "is the matter with you and your men?" "We are starving," said I, "and we must have something better than boiled corn." At the same time Cheek was brandishing his tomahawk over the pork barrel and clamoring for the "word." "Shall I break it open, Captain? Speak the word," he cried, while the rest of my crew were drawn up in line on the boat, with rifles, ready for action. The gentlemen *bourgeoises* yielded before this determined array and gave us a large supply of pork; that is, as much as we pleased to take. A few days after this we stopped to clean out the barges, and the pork in ours was removed to another and its place supplied with lead.

The Cheek who figured as ring-leader on this occasion was a Tennesseean, about six feet high and well-proportioned. His courage was equal

Cherokees. In 1820 he returned to his native Virginia, where he died in 1844.

to any enterprise, and his rashness and head-strong obstinacy at last, in the Indian country, cost him his life. I had on my barge a large, lazy, and very impertinent Irishman, who was frequently very sulky and remiss in his duties. I was compelled one day to call him by name for not working at the oars, saying to him he was not rowing the weight of his head. The height of disgrace among boatmen is to be publicly named by the Captain. The Irishman took my treatment in very ill humor and swore he would have satisfaction for the insult. When the boat stopped for breakfast, the men dispersed as usual to get wood, and with them went Cheek and my friend, the Irishman. Cheek returned without him and informed me he had whipped him "for saucing the Captain." I said: "Cheek I can attend to my own fighting without your assistance, or any other man's." "No, by G—d," said he, "my Captain shan't fight while I am about." The Irishman returned at length to the boat, but was so badly hurt as to be unable to work for several days.

The scenery of the Upper Missouri is so familiar to the world as to render any particular description unnecessary. As you ascend the river the woods diminish in number and extent. Beyond Council Bluffs, about 700 miles above the mouth, they entirely disappear, except on the river bottoms, which are heavily timbered. The prairies were covered with a short, thick grass, about three or four inches high. At this time the game was very abundant. We saw elk and buffaloes in vast numbers, and killed many of them. Prairie dogs and wolves were also very numerous. The Indians have thinned off the game since that time, so much that their own subsistence is frequently very scanty and they are often in danger of starvation. Their range for hunting now extends far down into the Comanche country and Texas, and the buffaloes, their only game of importance, are fast disappearing. When these valuable animals are all gone, when they are extinct on the west, as they are on the east side of the Mississippi, then will the Indian race, the aboriginals of that vast region, be near their own extinction and oblivion. They cannot survive the game and with it will disappear.[14]

The western declivity of the Mississippi Valley from the mountains to the Father of Waters is nearly all one great plain, with occasional rocky

[14]The practical extermination of the buffaloes a generation after these words were written is vividly narrated by John R. Cook, *The Border and the Buffalo*, the Lakeside Classics volume for 1938. The resistance offered by the Plains Indians to the destruction is described in Mrs. Margret I. Carrington's *Absaraka, Home of the Crows*, the Lakeside Classics volume for 1950, and in General George A. Custer's *My Life on the Plains*, the Lakeside Classics volume for 1952.

elevations. We saw hills at the foot of which were large heaps of pumice stone, which had the appearance of having been crumbled off from above by the action of fire. The scenery of Illinois or Missouri is a fair example of that of the whole country west to the mountains. The prairies here, however, are vaster and more desolate. One extensive plain is usually presented to the eye of the traveller, and stretches to the horizon, without a hill, mound, tree, or shrub to arrest the sight.[15]

We continued our ascent of the river without any occurrence of importance. Below Council Bluffs we met Captain Crooks,[16]

---

[15]Since James was traveling up the river in a boat, he lacked the opportunity to observe the Plains country more adequately. For a much better description of it, see General Custer's *My Life on the Plains.*

[16]This was Ramsay Crooks, notable for a generation as a leader of the American fur trade. Born in Scotland in 1787, he emigrated to Montreal at the age of sixteen and by 1806 had found his way to St. Louis. In 1807, in partnership with Robert McClelland, he set out with a party of 80 men for the Upper Missouri. En route they met Nathaniel Pryor's men returning down river from their defeat at the hands of the Arikaras, and abandoning the original design Crooks established a trading post near present-day Fort Calhoun, some twenty miles north of Omaha. In 1809, still but twenty-two years of age, he led a party of 40 men in the wake of the St. Louis Missouri Fur Company expedition, but abandoned the venture in consequence of the hostility of the Sioux. He was not connected with Astor's American Fur Company at this

agent for John J. Astor, who was trading with the Omahas.[17] Here all the few Americans remaining, with myself, were on the point of returning. By the solicitations and promises of the Company we were induced to continue with them.

The first Indians we saw were a party of Omahas hunting; with them were two Sioux chiefs. They sent forward a runner to their village above and themselves came on board our boats. We found the village at the mouth of the Jacques River, perhaps twelve hundred miles, by its course, from the mouth of the Missouri.[18] They

time. In 1810 the partnership with McClelland was dissolved and Crooks returned to Canada in time to join Astor's famous Astorian expedition. His activities as agent of Astor and as head of the American Fur Company subsequent to Astor's retirement from the fur trade in 1834 would require a volume to narrate. In 1856 he maintained that the band of Astorians which Robert Stuart conducted overland in 1812, and which Crooks accompanied, were the real discoverers of the noted South Pass of the Rockies.

[17]The Omaha tribe, of Siouan stock, was closely related to the Osage, Kansa, Ponca, and Quapaw tribes. In the historic period the Omaha had chiefly resided in eastern Nebraska, northward of the Platte to the vicinity of southern South Dakota. In 1802 an epidemic of small pox reduced the tribe to about 300 souls. It subsequently increased to about 1300 in 1850, remaining stationary thereafter for over half a century. In 1809, the population of the tribe must have been materially less than this figure.

[18]The James River of North and South Dakota, which enters the Missouri some ten miles below the city of Yankton.

were of the Teton tribe, which is kindred with the Sioux.[19] As we approached the bank, which was lined with hundreds, they fired into the water before the forward barge, and as we landed they retreated with great rapidity, making a startling noise with whistles and rattles.

After landing and making fast the boats, about fifty savages took charge of them, as a guard. They wore raven feathers on the head. Their bodies were naked, save about the middle, and painted entirely black. They presented, on the whole, a most martial and warlike appearance in their savage mode, and performed their office of guarding the boats so well that not even a chief was allowed to go onto them. Other Indians came with buffalo skins to be used as palanquins or litters for carrying the partners to their council house: each was taken up and carried off in state. I was compelled by some Indians to

---

[19]The Teton Sioux was the western division of the Sioux tribe, comprising over one-half its entire number. Included in it were the Oglala, Sans Arc, Minneconjou, Brulé and other sub-divisions. Among their leaders in the closing era of white-Indian warfare were such celebrated chiefs as Sitting Bull, Red Cloud, and Crazy Horse. They were the principal actors in all the nineteenth-century Indian wars of the northern Plains. In 1809 they were relatively unchanged by contact with the whites. As yet they had made no treaty with the United States, although they had participated in the wars of the Revolution and of 1812.

go in the same style to the place of council. Here
was a large company of old men awaiting us, and
for dinner we had served up a great feast of dog's
meat, a great delicacy with the Indians. The
rich repast was served in forty-one wooden
bowls, as I counted them, and from each bowl a
dog's foot was hanging out, evidently to prove
that this rarity was not a sham but a reality. Not
feeling very desirous of eating of this particular
dainty, I stole out and was pulled by a young
Indian and invited to his wigwam. I went and
partook with him of buffalo meat. We stayed with
these hospitable savages two days. On arriving,
we found the British flag flying, but easily persuaded them to haul it down. The Hudson's Bay
Company had had their emissaries among them
and were then dealing with them precisely as
they are now dealing with the savages in our
territory of Oregon—namely: buying them up
with presents and promises, and persuading them
to act as allies of Britain in any future war with
the United States.

On the third day we left the friendly Tetons
and proceeded up the river as before. Captain
Chouteau had conceived a prejudice against
Cheek, and on one occasion ordered him to leave
the boats. Lewis conveyed the order to me. I
remonstrated against the cruelty of sending a man
adrift in a wilderness, 1400 miles from home. He

insisted, and Cheek took his gun as if he was going to obey. Lewis ordered him to leave the gun behind, which he refused to do. Lewis then commanded me to take it from him. I replied that he or Chouteau might do that themselves. The men of my boat flew to their arms, and avowed their determination of defending Cheek and sharing his fate. The order was not pursued any further. Such rencounters and difficulties between the Americans and the partners embittered their hands against us, and ultimately did us no good. Much of the ill treatment we afterwards received from them was probably owing to the reckless assertion of our independence on every occasion and at every difficulty that occurred.

After leaving the Teton village our boat again failed of provisions, and by request of Lewis I went ashore on the north bank with one of our best hunters, named Brown, to kill some game. We went up the river and in the evening killed an elk, brought it to the river bank, and waited there for the boats till morning. They came up on the opposite shore and sent over a canoe to take us and our game across. The wind rose in the meantime and blew so strong as to raise the waves very high, and render it dangerous for us all to cross together in the same canoe. We sent over the game and Brown and myself con-

tinued our course afoot, expecting to get aboard
when the boats crossed at some one of the river
bends. By the middle of the day the wind had
risen so high that the boats, with sails hoisted,
quickly went out of sight. We travelled on till
evening and struck a large bayou, which we
could not cross, and took the backward course
till we encamped within a mile of the spot where
we had stayed the night before.

The next morning we struck off from the
river into the prairie and took the best course
we could to reach the boats. Seven days elapsed,
however, before we overtook them. The wind
blew a strong breeze and drove the boats along
very rapidly. We killed another elk and some
small game, which subsisted us till the fifth day,
when our amunition gave out. Our moccasins
being worn out fell off, and our feet were perfectly cut up by the prickly pear, which abounds
on these prairies. At last, nearly famished and
worn down, sore, lame, and exhausted, we
found the boats. My crew had, in vain, requested
leave to wait for us, and we might have perished
before the *bourgeoises* would have slackened their
speed in the least on our account. We had a
narrow escape from starvation on this excursion,
and I was ever afterwards careful to have plenty
of amunition with me when I went out, as I
frequently did, on similar expeditions.

In two days after this event we arrived at the country of the Arikaras. On approaching their village we took precautions against an attack. A guard marched along the shore, opposite to the boats, well armed. My crew composed a part of this force. When within half a mile of the village we drew up the cannon and prepared to encamp. The whole village came out in a body, as it seemed, to meet us. They had not come far toward us when an old chief rode out at full speed and with violent gestures and exclamations warned and motioned back his countrymen from before our cannon. The event of the year before was fresh in his recollection. He supposed we were about to inflict a proper and deserved punishment for the attack on Captain Pryor's troops and the murder of eight or ten of them, the year before. This old chief drove back all who were coming out to meet us. Captain Chouteau then sent for the chief to come down to his camp and hold a council. They refused to comply with this request and appeared very suspicious of our designs. After further negotiation, they agreed to come to us and hold a council if the Company's force would lay aside their arms and turn the cannon in the opposite direction. This was agreed to by the Company, with the provision that a guard should be on the ground, armed, during the conference. The council was held, and Chouteau harangued them on the crime committed against the government the year before. They promised better conduct for the future, but made no reparation, or apology even, for the past.

In a few days we started forward through a country marked by the same general features as that described before. Thousands of buffaloes covered the prairies on both sides of the river, making them black as far as the eye could reach. In ten or twelve days the boats reached the Mandan village, where I was awaiting them. I had sallied out five days before on a hunting excursion, and arrived at the village of the Mandans in advance of the boats. These are a poor, thieving, spiritless tribe, tributary to the Gros Ventres, who inhabit the country above them on the river.

The village is on the north side of the river.[20] The boats came up on the opposite shore. The wind, as they arrived, blew a hurricane and lashed

[20]The expedition arrived at the Mandan town on September 24, 1809. The sites of this village and that of the Gros Ventres were in the vicinity of the mouth of Knife River in west central North Dakota. In 1837 the Mandan nation was almost exterminated by an epidemic of small pox. For a vivid contemporary journal of this affliction see *Mississippi Valley Hist. Review*, XVII, 278–99. The neglect of the white visitors which the author comments upon was probably occasioned by their absorption in the return of their long-absent chief. Ordinarily the Mandans were distinctly friendly toward the whites.

the waves to a prodigious height. The Indians saw their chief, Shehaka, on our boats, and were almost frantic with joy and eagerness to speak with him. They have a round canoe made of hoops fastened together and a buffalo skin stretched over them, very light and portable. With these they rowed themselves across the turbulent river, one moment lost from view between the waves and the next riding over them like corks. In these tubs of canoes they crossed the stream to our boats. The natives made a jubilee and celebration for the return of Shehaka and neglected everything and everybody else. They hardly saw or took the least notice of their white visitors. The partners distributed the presents sent by the government and we then made haste to leave this boorish, inhospitable tribe.

We ascended the Missouri to the village of the Gros Ventres, on the south side of the river, fifteen miles above that of the Mandans. Here we found a far different race from the last; a manly, warlike, and independent tribe, who might well be called for their daring and enterprising qualities, the *Gros-Coeurs* or Big-Hearts, instead of Big Bellies. Here was our place of stopping for a short time, and of preparation for the business which had brought us hither. On our arrival at their village, four or five agents of the Hudson's Bay Company were among them, but they immediately crossed the river with their goods and bore off to the northeast.[21] We suspected them of inciting the Blackfeet against us, and many of our company attributed our subsequent misfortunes to their hostility. We afterwards heard that a large army of these Indians were encamped at the falls above. They traded regularly with the British traders and procured of them their arms and amunition.

We built a fort near the Gros Ventre village and unloaded all the larger boats for the purpose of sending them back to the settlements.[22] Hav-

[21]These men were agents, not of the Hudson's Bay Company, but of its bitter rival, the North West Company of Montreal.

[22]This fort should not be confused with Fort Lisa, built by Lisa about 16 miles above Bellevue, Nebraska. The present fort, long known as Manuel Lisa's fort, or the Missouri Fur Company fort, was on the west bank of the Missouri about 12 miles above Knife River. John Bradbury, the English traveler, who visited it in 1810, described it as consisting of a square block-house, the lower part of which was a room for furs, while the upper story was utilized as living quarters for Reuben Lewis and some of the hunters belonging to the establishment. There were some small outhouses, and the whole was surrounded by a 15-foot palisade. Attached to the fort was a "very pretty garden in which were peas, beans, sallad, radishes, and other vegetables, under the care of a gardener, an Irishman, who shewed it to me with much self-importance." Bradbury praised his management, but expressed his regret that there were no potatoes. "Oh, that does not signify," was the reply. "We can soon have them; there is plenty just over the way." Upon further

ing now arrived at our destination and being near the beaver region, we, the Americans, ten in number, requested the partners to furnish our traps, ammunition, guns, and men according to contract. But this they seemed to have forgotten entirely, or intended never to fulfil. We found ourselves taken in, cheated, chiseled, gulled, and swindled in a style that has not, perhaps, been excelled by Yankees or French, or men of any other nation, at any time in the thirty-six years that have passed over my head since this feat was performed. A stock of old and worthless traps had been brought up the river, apparently to be put off on the Americans. They offered us these traps, which we refused to take. They then endeavored to deprive us of the arms and ammunition belonging to them, in our possession, and they succeeded in getting from most of us all the guns and powder of theirs that we had.

Mine were taken from me, with the others, by order of the partners. I do not know that all of them consented to this nefarious proceeding. I hope and should have expected that several of

inquiry, Bradbury learned that "just over the way" was a post maintained by some British traders on the St. Peter's River of Minnesota, some 200 or 300 miles distant. R. G. Thwaites (Ed.), *Early Western Travels*, V, 156–57. Prince Maximilian who visited the place in 1833, found the fort had vanished but the site was still called "Manuel Lisa's fort."

them would not sanction such conduct. But I heard of no protest or opposition to the acts of the majority, who behaved toward us with a want of principle and of honor that would shame most gentleman robbers of the highway. They seemed determined to turn us out on the prairie and among the Indians without arms, provisions, or ammunition. Our situation, in that event, would have nearly realized the one implied in the popular expression, "a cat in hell without claws." We were kept waiting two or three weeks without employment or any provisions, except what we purchased at most exorbitant prices. We bought goods, knives, &c. of the Company on credit and sold them to the Indians for provisions and in this way were rapidly running in debt, which the Company expected us to discharge to them in beaver fur. Their object was to make the most out of us without regard to their previous professions and promises.

Finding myself, like most of my comrades, destitute of all means of support and sustenance, of defense and offense, I looked around for something by which I could live in that wild region. On arriving at the Gros Ventre village we had found a hunter and trapper named Colter, who had been one of Lewis & Clark's men, and had returned thus far with them in 1806. Of him I purchased a set of beaver traps for $120, a pound

and a half of powder for $6, and a gun for $40.
Seeing me thus equipped, Liza, the most active,
the meanest and most rascally of the whole, offered me new and good traps, a gun and ammunition. I told him he appeared willing enough to
help when help was not needed, and after I was,
provided at my own expense. I then selected two
companions, Miller and McDaniel, who had been
imposed on by the *bourgeoises* in the same manner
with myself, and in their company I prepared to
begin business. These two had, by good fortune,
brought with them six traps, two guns, and ammunition of their own. We cut down a tree and of
the trunk made a canoe in which we prepared to
ascend to the Forks and headwaters of the Missouri and the mountains. We were young and
sanguine of success. No fears of the future cloud-
ed our prospects and the adventures that lay before us excited our hopes and fancies to the highest pitch. No dangers daunted and no labors tired
us.

Before leaving the fort and my old companions,
I will relate a characteristic anecdote of Cheek,
who so soon after this expiated his follies by a
violent death. In an early part of the voyage,
when coming up the river about two months before, I had sent Cheek to draw our share of provisions from the provision boat. François Ride,
who dealt them out for the Company, offered

Cheek a bear's head, saying it was good enough for "you fellows," by this meaning the Americans. Cheek returned to his boat in a great rage at the insult, as he deemed it, and threatened to whip him (Ride) for the said contumely on himself and fellow companions, as soon as he was out of government employ—that is, as soon as we had delivered up Shehaka to the Mandans. The matter passed on and I supposed was forgotten by Cheek himself, until the fort was built and the Americans were about separating, with many grievances unredressed and wrongs unavenged. Cheek, meeting Ride one morning on the bank of the river, told him that he had promised to whip him and that he could not break his word on any account. He thereupon struck at the audacious Frenchman who had presumed to call Americans "fellows," and offer them a bear's head. Ride saved himself by running aboard one of the boats, where he obtained a reinforcement. Cheek beat a retreat, and a truce was observed by both parties till nightfall.

I had encamped with Cheek and two others a few hundred yards above the fort. We were all, except Cheek, in the tent, about nine o'clock in the evening, when Ride with a company, all armed with pistols and dirks, came up and demanded to see Cheek, saying that he had attacked him within the lines of the fort, when he knew he could not fight without violating orders. I told him that Cheek was not in the tent. "He is hid, the cowardly rascal," cried Ride, and went to searching the bushes. After he and his company were gone, I found Cheek at Major Henry's tent, amusing himself with cards and wine. I took him with me to our own tent, fearing that Ride's company might kill him if they found him that night. He was silent while hearing my account and for some minutes after entering our tent. He then spoke, as if on maturest reflection, and said that he had intended to have let Ride go with what he had got, "but now I will whip him in the morning if I lose my life by it."

In the morning he started, unarmed and wrapped in his blanket, for the fort. I with a few others followed to see fair play, which is ever a jewel with the American. Cheek soon found Ride and accosted him in front of the fort, informing him that he had came down to accommodate him with the interview which he had understood had been sought for so anxiously the night before. Ride said he was in liquor the night before, wanted to have nothing to do with him, and began to make for the fort. "You must catch a little any how," said Cheek, and springing towards Ride like a wild cat, with one blow he felled him to the earth. Captain Chouteau, who had seen the whole proceeding from the fort, immediately rushed out with about thirty of his men, all armed. "Bring out the irons, seize him, seize him!" cried Chouteau, frantic with passion and raging like a mad bull. Cheek prudently retired to our company on the bank of the river, a short distance, and said he would die rather than be ironed. We were ready to stand by him to the last. Chouteau now ordered his men to fire on us and the next moment would have seen blood-shed and the death of some of us had not Labbadie, Vallé, Menard, Morrison, Henry, and one of Chouteau's sons thrown themselves between us and the opposite party and thus prevented the execution of Chouteau's order.[23] Him they forced back, struggling like a mad child in its mother's arms, into the fort.

[23]These men were partners of the Fur Company. Jean Pierre Chouteau, military leader of the expedition, was a son of Pierre Laclede, founder of St. Louis. Born in 1758, he was brought to the new town as a child of six years by his mother, and until his death in 1849 St. Louis remained his home. He achieved wealth and prominence in the Indian trade, and until his retirement from active business in 1820 was one of the City's most influential citizens.

François Vallé was born December 8, 1779 at Ste. Genevieve, of which post his father was commandant. After several years passed in school in Newark, N.J. he returned to Missouri and about 1802 or 1803 went to the Upper Missouri on a trading expedition where he remained several years.

Pierre Menard was a native of Quebec who found his way to Kaskaskia in early manhood, where he soon became prominent. On the expedition of 1809 he served as a captain of infantry, and following the delivery of Shehaka

On the next day after this fracas, Miller, Mc-
Daniel, and myself parted from our companions,
after agreeing to meet them again on the Forks or
headwaters of the Missouri, and started in our
canoe up the river. The river is very crooked in
this part and much narrower than we had found
it below. We came to a Mandan village on the
south side of the stream on the day of our departure from the fort. On arriving here, we were on

to his tribe Menard and Andrew Henry, early in 1810,
led the company of trappers to Three Forks of the Missouri. Driven off by the Blackfeet, Henry crossed the
Rockies to the Upper Snake, while Menard returned to
Kaskaskia. He held several public offices, and until his
death in 1844 enjoyed practically universal esteem. Menard County, Illinois, was named for him and in 1866 a
statue in his honor was erected on the State Capitol
grounds in Springfield.

William Morrison was a Pennsylvanian, born in 1763,
who removed to the French Illinois in early manhood,
where he soon became an influential citizen. As western
partner of his uncle, Guy Bryan of Philadelphia, he directed the merchandising activities of the firm throughout
a vast area of country. In 1804 he undertook to open a trade
with New Mexico by sending Baptiste Lalande to Santa Fe.

Andrew Henry, another Pennsylvanian, was born about
1775. He came to Upper Louisiana in 1800. To escape
the Blackfeet, who were harassing the party Henry and
Menard led to Three Forks in 1810, Henry with a portion
of the command crossed the mountains, where they win-
tered (1810–11) on Henry's Fork of Snake River, returning to St. Louis the following season. In 1822 he re-
sumed the fur trade, this time in association with William
H. Ashley. After wintering at the mouth of the Yellowstone, he pushed farther west, only once more to be at-

the north side of the river, and on account of the
violence of the wind did not cross to the village.
Late in the evening a woman in attempting to
cross in a skin canoe was overset in the middle of
the river. She was seen from the village, and immediately a multitude of men rushed into the
water and seemed to run rather than swim to the
woman, whom they rescued from the water with
wonderful rapidity. Their dexterity in swimming
was truly astonishing to us. We pushed or rather
paddled on in a shower of rain till late that night
and encamped. In the morning we went on in a
snow-storm and in four days the ice floating in
the river prevented further navigation of the
stream with the canoe.

tacked and defeated by the Blackfeet near Great Falls,
Montana. Several subsequent expeditions were undertaken, which we do not pause to recount. His later years
were devoted to mining activities. He died at his Washington County, Missouri, home, June 10, 1833.

Sylvestre Labbadie was born in St. Louis, February 19,
1779, and at this time was in his thirty-first year. In 1800,
when he was but twenty-one, he petitioned the Spanish
government for a land grant of some 14,000 acres in
present-day Franklin County, Missouri. He was successful, and the title was subsequently confirmed by the
American government. The town of Labbadie is situated
on this grant. In 1806 Labbadie married a member of the
powerful Chouteau clan. He passed his life as a business
man in St. Louis, and among other activities is reputed
to have built the City's first saw-mill in 1818. He became
wealthy and retired from active business at an early age.
He died, July 25, 1849.

We stopped on the south side of the river, built a small cabin, banked it round with earth, and soon made ourselves quite comfortable. This was in the month of November. We had caught a few beaver skins on our route from the Gros Ventre village, and employed ourselves in making moccasins and leggins and in killing game, which was very plenty all around us. Here we determined to pass the winter and in the spring continue our ascent of the Missouri to the Forks. On Christmas day I froze my feet and became so disabled as to be confined to the house, unable to walk. Miller and McDaniel soon after started back for the fort with our stock of beaver skins to exchange them for ammunition. They were gone twice the length of time agreed on for their stay. I began to consume the last of my rations and should have suffered for food had not a company of friendly Indians called at the cabin and bartered provisions for trinkets and tobacco.

My next visitors were two Canadians and an American named Ayers, from the fort, who were going on with despatches for the main Company, that was supposed to be at Manuel's fort at the mouth of the Big Horn, a branch of the Yellowstone. These men informed me that Miller and McDaniel had changed their mind: that they did not intend to continue farther up the river, and seemed to be in no haste to return to me. They

urged me to accompany them, and promised me
the use of one of their horses till my feet should
become well enough for me to walk. I consented
to go with them and prepared to leave my cabin.
Before doing so I buried the traps and other
accouterments of my two former companions in a
corner of the lodge, and peeling off the bark from
a log above them, I wrote on it: "In this corner
your things lie" I learned on my return in the
spring that both of them had been killed, as was
supposed by the Arikaras. Their guns, traps, &c.
were seen in the hands of some of that tribe, but
they were never heard of afterwards.

On the third of February, 1810, eight months
after my departure from St. Louis, I started from
my winter lodge, but I soon repented my under-
taking. The horses were all too weak to carry
more than the load appropriated to them, and I
was thus compelled to walk. My feet became very
sore and gave me great pain, while the crust on
the snow made the travelling of all of us both
slow and difficult. I suffered severely at starting
but gradually improved in strength and was able
in a few days to keep up with less torture to myself than at first. We ascended the south bank of
the river till we struck the Little Missouri, a
branch from the south. Here we found some Indians who advised us to keep up the banks of this
river for two days, and then, turning northward-

ly, a half day's travel would bring us to the Gun-
powder River near its head. This is a branch of
the Yellowstone.

We travelled two days as directed and left the
Little Missouri in search of the river.[24] We missed
it entirely, on account of our travelling so much
slower than the Indians are accustomed to do.
Our two days' travel was not greater than one of
theirs. For five days we kept our course to the
north in an open plain, and in the heart of winter.
The cold was intense, and the wind from the
mountains most piercing. The snow blew directly
in our faces and ice was formed on our lips and
eyebrows. In this high latitude and in the open
prairies in the vicinity of the mountains, where
we then were, the winters are very cold. On the
first night we were covered where we lay to the

---

[24]The directions given by the Indians were quite impossible, as the party was now to discover to its sorrow.
The Little Missouri, in its lower course, flows some seventy miles due east to its junction with the Missouri.
Since James' party traveled slowly, it probably turned
northward in search of the Powder at some point of this
seventy-mile stretch. But the Powder lay still 100 miles
or more to the Southwest. Precisely where James and his
companions wandered upon leaving the Little Missouri
can only be surmised. They had been told by the Indians
to travel north, which would have brought them to the
Missouri shortly below or above the mouth of the Yellowstone. Eventually, as the narrative shows, they ascended the Yellowstone to Lisa's establishment at the
mouth of the Big Horn.

depth of three feet by the snow. No game was to be seen and we were destitute of provisions. For five days we tasted not a morsel of food, and had not even the means of making a fire. We saw not a mound or hill, tree or shrub, not a beast nor a bird, until the fifth day, when we descried afar off a high mound. We were destitute, alone in that vast, desolate, and to us limitless, expanse of drifting snow, which the winds drove into our faces and heaped around our steps.

Snow was our only food and drink, and snow made our covering at night. We suffered dreadfully from hunger. On the first and second days after leaving the Little Missouri for the desert we were now traversing, our appetites were sharper and the pangs of hunger more intense than afterwards. A languor and faintness succeeded, which made travelling most laborious and painful. On the fifth day we had lost so much strength and felt such weakness for want of food that the most terrible of deaths, a death by famine, stared us in the face. The pangs and miseries we endured are vividly described by Mr. Kendall, from actual experience, in his *Santa Fe Expedition*.[25]

[25]George W. Kendall's *Narrative of the Texan Santa Fe Expedition* . . . was first published by the Harper Brothers, New York, in a two-volume edition of over 800 pages. The first volume and Chapter I of the second were reprinted as the Lakeside Classics volume for 1929, the length of the original narrative being too great for in-

My feet, in addition to all other sufferings, now became sore and more painful than ever. The men had made for me a moccasin of skin taken from the legs of a buffalo, which I wore with the hair next to my feet and legs. I felt the blood gurgling and bubbling in this casing at every step. We were about to ward off starvation by killing a horse and eating the raw flesh and blood, when on the fifth day of our wandering in this wilderness a mound was seen, as above mentioned, in the distance. We reached and ascended it in the evening, whence we saw woods and buffaloes before us. We hastened to kill several of these noblest of all game animals, and encamped in the woods, where we quickly made a fire and cut up the meat.

We were all so voracious in our appetites as not to wait for the cooking, but ate great quantities nearly raw. The first taste stimulated our languor and appetites to an ungovernable pitch. We ate, and ate, and ate, as if there were no limit to our capacity, and no quantity could satisfy us. At length, when gorged to the full and utterly unable to hold any more, we gave out and sought repose about midnight under our tents. But sleep fled from our eyes, and in the morning we arose

clusion in its entirety in the series. Chapter 12, entitled "Starvation and relief" (pp. 356–58) contains the description of starvation to which James alludes.

without having rested, feverish and more fatigued than when we supped and retired the night before. Our feet, limbs, and bodies were swollen and bloated, and we all found ourselves laid up on the sick list by our debauch on buffalo meat.

We had no desire to eat again on that day, and remained in camp, utterly unable to travel, till the next morning, when we started forward, travelling slowly. We soon struck the river, which we had suffered so much in seeking, and bent our course up the stream, crossing its bends on the ice. On one occasion, when saving distance by cutting off a bend of the river, the horse carrying my pack and worldly goods fell into an air hole and would have instantly disappeared had I not caught him by the tail and dragged him out to some distance, with a risk to myself of plunging under the ice into a rapid current that made me shudder the moment I coolly looked at the danger. Hair-breadth escapes from death are so frequent in the life of a hunter in this wild region as to lose all novelty and may seem unworthy of mention. I shall relate a few as I proceed, for the purpose of showing the slight tenure the pioneer holds of life. And yet Boone, the prince of the prairies, "lived hunting up to ninety." Perhaps pure air and continual exercise are more than a counterbalance toward a long life, against all the dangers of a hunter's and trapper's existence, even among hostile savages, such as we were now rapidly approaching.

We continued our course up the Yellowstone, gradually recovering from the effects of our unnatural surfeit and gross gormandizing of buffalo meat. The country here is one immense, level plain, and abounded, at this time, with large herds of buffaloes, which subsisted on the buds of trees and the grass which the powerful winds laid bare of snow in many places. The river was skirted on either side by woods. At last, after fifteen days of painful travel and much suffering, we reached Manuel's fort at the mouth of the Big Horn, where I found the most of my crew and a small detachment of the Company's men, from whom I had parted the previous fall. This fort, as before mentioned, was built by Lisa in the spring of 1808 and a small garrison left in it, who had remained there ever since.

Here I found Cheek, Brown, Dougherty,[26] and the rest of my crew rejoicing to see me. I was not

[26]John Dougherty was born in Kentucky. When but seventeen years old he migrated to St. Louis and in 1809 joined the Upper Missouri expedition of the St. Louis Missouri Fur Company. In 1820 he was appointed U.S. Indian agent with headquarters at Fort Leavenworth. Although his station was several times removed, he continued in this office until 1837. The remainder of his life was passed as a resident of Clay County, Missouri, where he died at the age of seventy in 1861. A long and appreciative eulogy by his friend and fellow townsman

a little surprised to find Col. Pierre Menard in command, who was to have returned to St. Louis from the fort at the Gros Ventre village, and Lisa intended to take command of the party on the headwaters of the Missouri. Such was the arrangement at the commencement of the voyage. I soon learned from the men what they supposed to be the cause of the change. The next day after I left the fort on the Missouri, in the fall, Cheek and several Americans were in the office or *marquee* of the Company, endeavoring to get their equipments according to contract. Lisa was present. Chouteau's name was mentioned in the course of the conversation, when Cheek coolly remarked that if he caught Chouteau a hundred yards from camp he would shoot him. "Cheek! Cheek!!" ex-

General Alexander W. Doniphan, published in the Liberty *Tribune*, Jan. 4, 1861, is reprinted by Douglas, pp. 279–81. In it, Doniphan states that Dougherty, by his many years passed in the Indian country, possessed a fuller knowledge of the "habits, manners, tasks, and peculiarities" of the northwestern Indians, and a greater influence over them, than any other white man had ever acquired; "this did not result so much from his peculiar knowledge of them as it did from the man himself—his face, his physique, were perfect; a bright and intellectual eye; and unvarying candor and directness in all his intercourse with them, at once pleased, charmed, and overawed them."

After this characterization of the well-nigh perfect Indian agent, one is saddened to read that Dougherty was dismissed from office to make room for a victorious "spoils" successor.

claimed Lisa, "mind what you say." "I do that," said Cheek, "and Lisa, I have heard some of our boys say that if they ever caught you two hundred yards from camp they would shoot you, and if they don't I will. You ought not to expect anything better from the Americans after having treated them with so much meanness, treachery, and cruelty as you have. Now Lisa," continued he, "you are going to the Forks of the Missouri. Mark my words, you will never come back alive." Lisa's cheeks blanched at this bold and reckless speech from a man who always performed his promises, whether good or evil. He returned to St. Louis and sent up Col. Menard in his place.

Col. M. was an honorable, high-minded gentleman, and he enjoyed our esteem in a higher degree than any other member of the Company. Lisa we thoroughly detested and despised, both for his acts and his reputation. There were many tales afloat concerning villainies said to have been perpetrated by him on the frontiers. These may have been wholly false or greatly exaggerated, but in his looks there was no deception. Rascality sat on every feature of his dark-complexioned, Mexican face—gleamed from his black, Spanish eyes, and seemed enthroned in a forehead "villainous low." We were glad to be relieved of his presence.

After remaining at this fort or camp a few days we started westward for the Forks and mountains in a company of thirty-two men, French and Americans. On first arriving at the fort I had learned that two of the men with an Indian chief of the Snake tribe and his two wives and a son had gone forward with the intention of killing game for our company and awaiting our approach on the route. Our second day's journey brought us to an Indian lodge; stripped, and near by, we saw a woman and boy lying on the ground, with their heads split open, evidently by a tomahawk. These were the Snake's elder wife and son, he having saved himself and his younger wife by flight on horseback. Our two men who had started out in company with him were not molested. They told us that a party of Gros Ventres had come upon them, committed these murders, and passed on, as if engaged in a lawful and praiseworthy business.

These last were the most powerful and warlike Indians of that region. The poor Snake tribe, on the contrary, were the weakest, and consequently became the prey and victims of the others. They inhabit the caves and chasms of the mountains and live a miserable and precarious life in eluding the pursuit of enemies. All the neighboring tribes were at war with these poor devils. Every party we met pretended to be out on an expedition against the Snakes, whom they frequently reduce to slavery.[27] Thus the strong prey upon the weak in savage as well as in civilized life.

Our course now lay to the northwest for the Forks of the Missouri, which meet in latitude— among the mountains, whence the last named river runs directly north as high as latitude— miles, where it turns to the south and southeast, which last course it generally holds to its junction with the Mississippi. On the evening of the day when we left Manuel's fort my friend Brown became blind from the reflection of the sun on the snow; his eyes pained him so much that he implored us to put an end to his torment by shooting him. I watched him during that night for fear he would commit the act himself. He complained that his eyeballs had bursted, and moaned and groaned most piteously. In the morning I opened the swollen lids, and informed him to his great joy that the balls were whole and sound. He could now distinguish a faint glimmering of light. I led him all that day and the next. On the third he

[27]The name "Snake" was loosely applied, in the period of early white contact, to certain subdivisions of the widespread Shoshonean family, whose culture ranged from the lowly Digger Indians of the Great Basin to the settled Hopi of New Mexico and the Comanche, Bannock, and other game-hunting tribes east of the Rockies. More particularly, it was attached to the natives of eastern Oregon. One notable member of the Snake, or Shoshone, family was Sacajawea, heroine of the Lewis and Clark expedition.

had so far recovered that he could see, though but indistinctly.

Our guide on this route was Colter, who thoroughly knew the road, having twice escaped over it from capture and death at the hands of the Indians.[28] In ten or twelve days after leaving the fort we entered an opening or gap in the mountains, where it commenced snowing most violently and so continued all night. The morning showed us the heads and backs of our horses just

[28] John Colter was a Virginian who joined the Lewis and Clark expedition at Louisville in 1803. He proved to be one of its most reliable members. When the expedition arrived at Fort Mandan on its return journey in the summer of 1806, Colter asked to be discharged in order to join with another trapper in a two-year hunt for beaver skins, "determined," as Sergeant Ordway wrote, "to stay until they made a fortune." Much of Colter's further activities are related by our author. In 1807–1808, sent by Lisa on a lone mission to the Blackfeet at the mouth of the Big Horn, Colter visited the Yellowstone Park area and became the white discoverer of this natural wonderland. Despite his indifference to danger, Colter eventually became surfeited and in 1810 returned to Missouri, where he married and settled upon a farm near the present-day hamlet of Dundee in Franklin County. He died in November, 1813. James' subsequent relation of Colter's thrilling escape is one of two contemporary accounts obtained directly from Colter. For the other, see John Bradbury's *Travels*, reprinted by Thwaites (Ed.), *Early Western Travels*, V, 44–47. Bradbury's account was obtained from Colter upon the arrival of the latter at St. Louis in the spring of 1810. A recent biography of Colter by Burton Harris is *John Colter: His Years in the Rockies*, (New York, 1952).

visible above the snow, which had crushed down all our tents. We proceeded on with the greatest difficulty. As we entered the ravine or opening of the mountain the snow greatly increased in depth, being in places from fifty to sixty feet on the ground, a third of which had fallen and drifted in that night. The wind had heaped it up in many places to a prodigious height. The strongest horses took the front to make a road for us, but soon gave out and the ablest-bodied men took their places as pioneers. A horse occasionally stepped out of the beaten track and sank entirely out of sight in the snow. By night we had made about four miles for that day's travel. By that night we passed the ravine and reached the Gallatin River, being the eastern fork of the Missouri.[29] The river sweeps rapidly by the pass at its western extremity, on each side of which the mountains rise perpendicularly from the bank of the river and apparently stopped our progress up and down the east side of the stream. I forded it and was followed by Dougherty, Weir[30] and

---

[29]The party had crossed by way of the Bozeman Pass from the Upper Yellowstone in the general vicinity of Livingston to the Gallatin, the easterly member of the trio of rivers which converge at Three Forks to form the Missouri. Present-day U.S. Highway No. 10 parallels their route more or less closely.

[30]This was William Weir, another Kentuckian, who removed to Missouri in early manhood and in 1809 joined

another, when Colter discovered an opening through the mountain on the right or north side, and through it led the rest of the company. We, however, proceeded down the left bank of the river till night, when we encamped and supped (four of us) on a piece of buffalo meat about the size of the two hands.

During this and the preceding day we suffered from indistinct vision, similar to Brown's affliction on leaving the Big Horn. We all now became blind, as he had been, from the reflection of the sun's rays on the snow. The hot tears trickled from the swollen eyes, nearly blistering the cheeks, and the eyeballs seemed bursting from our heads. At first, the sight was obscured as by a silk veil or handkerchief, and we were unable to hunt. Now we could not even see our way before us, and in this dreadful situation we remained two days and nights. Hunger was again inflicting its sharp pangs upon us and we were upon the point of killing one of the packhorses when on the fourth day after crossing the Gallatin one of the men killed a goose, of which, being now somewhat re-

the expedition about to set out for the Upper Missouri. He remained in the Upper Country several years and is characterized by Douglas as "an active, efficient man, brave and skillful," who ranked with Dougherty and Colter. After about a decade he settled in Missouri, living in Cooper and (later) Crawford counties. He died at his home in 1845.

covered from our blindness, we made a soup and stayed the gnawings of hunger. The next day our eyes were much better, and we fortunately killed an elk, of which we ate without excess, being taught by experience the dangers of gluttony after a fast.

We continued on down the river and soon came in sight of our comrades in the main body on the right bank. They, like ourselves, had all been blind, and had suffered more severely than we from the same causes. They had killed three dogs, one a present to me from an Indian, and two horses to appease the demands of hunger, before they had sufficiently recovered to take sight on their guns. While in this distressed situation, enveloped by thick darkness at midday, thirty Snake Indians came among them and left without committing any depredation. Brown and another, who suffered less than the others, saw and counted these Indians, who might have killed them all and escaped with their effects with perfect impunity. Their preservation was wonderful. When we overtook them they were slowly recovering from blindness, and we all encamped together with thankful and joyous hearts for our late narrow escape from a painful and lingering death.[31]

[31]Lieutenant James H. Bradley, an intelligent and scholarly soldier of the seventies in Montana, records this account of his own experience with snow blindness:

"I had designed to rejoin the command with my prisoners [two deserters, of whom he had been sent in pursuit] but found on getting up and going into the light that I was a victim of snow-blindness. I had gone to the jail to give orders about my prisoners when I discovered my sight failing and was scarcely able to reach the hotel ere I became totally blind. The loss of sight came with a feeling such as is created by smoke in the eyes, that, if the case is a severe one, soon increases into the most intense burning pain. The eyes cannot bear the light and the eyeballs seem to roll in liquid fire with a grating feeling as though in contact with particles of sand. The temptation to bandage them or apply water is great, but should be resisted, as the one heats the eyes and the other increases the irritation, and the pain is only intensified. This blindness seems mainly confined to high altitudes, but I have heard of occasional cases as far south as the plains of western Kansas ... The Indians and even wild animals are subject to it, and to the frequenter of our western Plains a snow-blind rabbit or even a sage or prairie chicken is no uncommon sight. A method of treatment practiced by some of the northwestern Indians is to drop into the corner of the eye a little skunk oil, which they extract and preserve for this purpose. I have been assured by old hunters who have tried it that it is a sovereign remedy. But prevention is infinitely preferable to cure, and may be effected by blackening the face to the depth of an inch or more around the eyes close up to the lids ... A bit of wet powder or lampblack, the soot off the bottom of a kettle, a charred stick, or powdered charcoal will accomplish this. ... In the month of May, 1867 I had 30 men out of a command of 40 disabled in this manner as the result of one day's march through the snow on a sunny day, myself being the greatest sufferer as my duties compelled me to use my eyes most. The number of the well was barely sufficient to attend to the afflicted, and we lay several days almost defenseless in an Indian country." Bradley's Journal. March 19, 1876, in Montana Hist. Soc., *Contributions*, II, 143-44.

We proceeded on in better spirits. On the next day we passed a battlefield of the Indians, where the skulls and bones were lying around on the ground in vast numbers. The battle which had caused this terrible slaughter took place in 1808, the year but one before, between the Blackfeet[32] to the number of fifteen hundred on the one side, and the Flatheads and Crows, numbering together about eight hundred, on the other. Colter

[32]The Blackfoot Confederacy included the Blackfoot, Piegan, and Blood tribes. They occupied much of the area stretching from the North Saskatchewan River to the headwaters of the Missouri and from about the Montana-North Dakota border westward to the Rockies. Possession of the region was sharply contested by the Crows, Sioux, and other tribes, with which they fought more or less continually. When Lewis and Clark were returning from the Pacific in the summer of 1806 Lewis had an encounter with a small horse stealing band of Blackfeet in which two of them were killed. Although some writers attribute the subsequent hostility of the tribe to the whites to this incident, others with more probability attribute it to subsequent encounters, the first of these being the battle of 1808 between the Crows and the Blackfeet in which Colter more or less innocently figured. He had been sent by Lisa on the lone mission already noted (*ante, p. 47.*) to the forks of the Missouri to find the Blackfeet and invite them to come to Lisa's fort to trade. En route he fell in with a band of Crows, which was presently attacked by the Blackfeet. The latter, defeated in the encounter, and seeing a white man fighting in the ranks of the enemy, conceived a settled hostility toward the Americans. Letter of Major Thomas Biddle to Gen. Henry Atkinson, Oct. 29, 1819, in *Am. State Papers, Indian Aff.*, II, 201.

was in the battle on the side of the latter, and was wounded in the leg, and thus disabled from standing. He crawled to a small thicket and there loaded and fired while sitting on the ground. The battle was desperately fought on both sides, but victory remained with the weaker party. The Blackfeet engaged at first with about five hundred Flatheads, whom they attacked in great fury. The noise, shouts, and firing brought a reinforcement of Crows to the Flatheads, who were fighting with great spirit and defending the ground manfully. The Blackfeet, who are the Arabs of this region, were at length repulsed, but retired in perfect order and could hardly be said to have been defeated. The Flatheads are a noble race of men, brave, generous and hospitable. They might be called the Spartans of Oregon.[33] Lewis and Clark had received much kindness from them in their expedition to the Columbia, which waters their

[33]The term Flatheads has been loosely applied to numerous tribes, ranging from the Choctaw and the Catawba of the Southwestern United States to the Chinook and allied tribes of the Lower Columbia Basin. The tribe to which James applies the name were the Salish, who dwelt on the upper waters of the Columbia, frequently crossing the mountains in pursuit of game, when they became the prey of the Blackfoot and other Plains-dwelling tribes. Despite their name, they did not practice the head-flattening custom followed by the tribes of the Lower Columbia. Instead, they were called Flatheads because, in contrast to these tribes, they left their heads in their natural condition, which thus were flat on top.

country, and at the time of this well-fought battle Colter was leading them to Manuel's fort to trade with the Americans, when the Blackfeet fell upon them in such numbers as seemingly to make their destruction certain. Their desperate courage saved them from a general massacre.

The following day we reached the long sought Forks of the Missouri, or the place of confluence of the Gallatin, Madison, and Jefferson rivers. Here at last after ten months of travel we encamped, commenced a fort in the point made by the Madison and Jefferson forks, and prepared to begin business.[34] This point was the scene of

---

[34]Lieutenant James H. Bradley, whose journal is quoted *ante*, note 31, wrote on March 26, 1876: "Within sight of our camp the mighty Missouri takes its rise ... Both from this circumstance and from the history connected with it, the locality is one of the most interesting in Montana, it being here that the first fur trading establishment on the Upper Missouri stood ... I was aware of the existence of this old fort and knew something of its history, and was therefore induced to pass the afternoon making personal search and diligent inquiry after any possible remaining traces of it that would indicate the spot where it had stood. Toward night I found what I had sought, but too late to make personal examination of the little that remains. The good people of that neighborhood call it 'Lewis and Clark's Fort,' and relate to the interested inquirer how these famous captains passed a winter in it on their way across the continent, concealing in a cache nearby a large amount of valuable property. This fabled cache has given rise to an investigating spirit almost equal to that once displayed in the search for the buried treas-

Colter's escape in the fall of the year but one before, from the Indians and a death by torture; an event so extraordinary and thrilling, as he related it to me, that it deserves a brief narration.

ure of Captain Kidd, and a deal of useless digging has been done in the neighborhood.

"In 1870 the outlines of the fort were still intact, from which it appears that it was a double stockade of logs set three feet deep, enclosing an area of about 300 feet square, situated upon the tongue of land (at that point half a mile wide) between the Jefferson and Madison rivers about two miles above their confluence, upon the south bank of a channel now called Jefferson Slough. Since then the stream has made such inroads upon the land that only a small portion of the fort—the southwest angle—remains." Thus pass the works of man. Lieutenant Bradley, a valiant soldier who both made and wrote Montana history, was killed in the Battle of the Big Hole a year later, August 9, 1877.

CHAPTER II

Trapping Beaver and Fighting Blackfeet

WHEN Colter was returning in 1807 with Lewis and Clark from Oregon he met a company of hunters ascending the Missouri, by whom he was persuaded to return to the trapping region, to hunt and trap with them. Here he was found by Lisa in the following year, whom he assisted in building the fort at the Big Horn. In one of his many excursions from this post to the Forks of the Missouri for beaver, he made the wonderful escape adverted to in the last chapter, which I give precisely as he related it to me. His veracity was never questioned among us and his character was that of a true American backwoodsman. He was about thirty-five years of age, five feet ten inches in height, and wore an open, ingenuous, and pleasing countenance of the Daniel Boone stamp. Nature had formed him, like Boone, for hardy endurance of fatigue, privations, and perils.

He had gone with a companion named Potts to the Jefferson River, which is the most western of the Three Forks, and runs near the base of the mountains. They were both proceeding up the river in search of beaver, each in his own canoe, when a war party of about eight hundred Blackfoot Indians suddenly appeared on the east bank of the river. The chiefs ordered them to come ashore, and apprehending robbery only and knowing the utter hopelessness of flight, and having dropped his traps over the side of the canoe from the Indians into the water, which was here quite shallow, he hastened to obey their mandate. On reaching the shore he was seized, disarmed, and stripped entirely naked. Potts was still in his canoe in the middle of the stream, where he remained stationary, watching the result. Colter requested him to come ashore, which he refused to do, saying he might as well lose his life at once as to be stripped and robbed in the manner Colter had been. An Indian immediately fired and shot him about the hip; he dropped down in the canoe, but instantly rose with his rifle in his hands. "Are you hurt," said Colter. "Yes," said he, "too much hurt to escape; if you can get away, do so. I will kill at least one of them." He leveled his rifle and shot an Indian dead. In an instant at least a hundred bullets pierced his body, and as many savages rushed into the stream and pulled the canoe, containing his riddled corpse, ashore. They dragged the body up onto the bank and with their hatchets and knives cut and hacked it all to pieces, and limb from limb. The entrails, heart, lungs, &c., they threw into Colter's face. The relations of the killed Indian were furious with rage and struggled, with tomahawk in hand, to reach Colter, while others held them back. He was every moment expecting the death blow or the fatal shot that should lay him beside his companion. A council was hastily held over him and his fate quickly determined upon.

He expected to die by torture, slow, lingering, and horrible. But they had magnanimously determined to give him a chance, though a slight one, for his life. After the council a chief pointed to the prairie and motioned him away with his hand, saying in the Crow language, "go—go away." He supposed they intended to shoot him as soon as he was out of the crowd and presented a fair mark to their guns. He started in a walk and an old Indian, with impatient signs and exclamations, told him to go faster, and as he still kept a walk the same Indian manifested his wishes by still more violent gestures and adjurations. When he had gone a distance of eighty or a hundred yards from the army of his enemies he saw the younger Indians throwing off their blankets, leggins, and other incumbrances, as if for a race. Now he knew their object. He was to run a race, of which the prize was to be his own life and scalp.

Off he started with the speed of the wind. The war-whoop and yell immediately arose behind him, and looking back he saw a large company of young warriors, with spears, in rapid pursuit. He ran with all the strength that nature, excited to the utmost, could give; fear and hope lent a supernatural vigor to his limbs, and the rapidity of his flight astonished himself. The Madison Fork lay directly before him, five miles from his starting place. He had run half the distance when his strength began to fail and the blood to gush from his nostrils. At every leap the red stream spurted before him, and his limbs were growing rapidly weaker and weaker. He stopped and looked back; he had far outstripped all his pursuers and could get off if his strength would only hold out. One solitary Indian, far ahead of the others, was rapidly approaching, with a spear in his right hand and a blanket streaming behind from his left hand and shoulder.

Despairing of escape, Colter awaited his pursuer and called to him in the Crow language to save his life. The savage did not seem to hear him, but letting go his blanket and seizing his spear with both hands he rushed at Colter, naked and defenseless as he stood before him, and made a desperate lunge to transfix him. Colter seized the spear near the head with his right hand, and exerting his whole strength, aided by the weight of the falling Indian, who had lost his balance in the fury of the onset, he broke off the iron head or blade which remained in his hand, while the savage fell to the ground and lay prostrate and disarmed before him. Now was *his* turn to beg for his life, which he did in the Crow language, and held up his hands imploringly, but Colter was not in a mood to remember the golden rule, and pinned his adversary through the body to the earth by one stab with the spear head. He quickly drew the weapon from the body of the now dying Indian, and seizing his blanket as lawful spoil, he again set out with renewed strength, feeling, he said to me, as if he had not run a mile. A shout and yell arose from the pursuing army in his rear as from a legion of devils, and he saw the prairie behind him covered with Indians in full and rapid chase.

Before him, if anywhere, was life and safety; behind him, certain death; and running as never man before sped the foot, except, perhaps, at the Olympic Games, he reached his goal, the Madison River, and the end of his five-mile heat. Dashing through the willows on the bank, he plunged into the stream and saw close beside him a beaver house, standing like a coal-pit about ten feet above the surface of the water, which was here of about the same depth. This presented to him a refuge from his ferocious enemies, of which he immediately availed himself. Diving under the water he arose into the beaver house, where he found a dry and comfortable resting place on the upper floor or story of this singular structure.

The Indians soon came up, and in their search for him they stood upon the roof of his house of refuge, which he expected every moment to hear them breaking open. He also feared that they would set it on fire. After a diligent search on that side of the river, they crossed over, and in about two hours returned again to his temporary habitation, in which he was enjoying bodily rest, though with much anxious foreboding. The beaver houses are divided into two stories and will generally accommodate several men in a dry and comfortable lodging. In this asylum Colter kept fast till night. The cries of his terrible enemies had gradually died away and all was still around him when he ventured out of his hiding place by the same opening under the water by which he had entered and which admits the beavers to their building.

He swam the river and hastened towards the mountain gap or ravine, about thirty miles above on the river, through which our company passed in the snow with so much difficulty. Fearing that the Indians might have guarded this pass, which was the only outlet from the valley, and to avoid the danger of a surprise, Colter ascended the almost perpendicular mountain before him, the tops and sides of which a great way down were covered with perpetual snow. He clambered up this fearful ascent about four miles below the gap, holding on by the rocks, shrubs, and branches of trees, and by morning had reached the top. He lay there concealed all that day, and at night proceeded on in the descent of the mountain, which he accomplished by dawn. He now hastened on in the open plain towards Manuel's fort on the Big Horn, about three hundred miles ahead in the northeast. He travelled day and night, stopping only for necessary repose and eating roots and the bark of trees, for eleven days. He reached the fort, nearly exhausted by hunger, fatigue, and excitement. His only clothing was the Indian's blanket, whom he had killed in the race, and his only weapon the same Indian's spear, which he brought to the fort as a trophy. His beard was long, his face and whole body were thin and emaciated by hunger, and his limbs and feet swollen and sore. The company at the fort did not recognize him in this dismal plight until he had made himself known.

Colter, now with me, passed over the scene of his capture and wonderful escape, and described his emotions during the whole adventure with great minuteness. Not the least of his exploits was the scaling of the mountain, which seemed to me impassable, even by the mountain goat. As I looked at its rugged and perpendicular sides I wondered how he ever reached the top, a feat probably never performed before by mortal man.

The whole affair is a fine example of the quick and ready thoughtfulness and presence of mind in a desperate situation, and the power of endurance, which characterize the western pioneer. As we passed over the ground where Colter ran his race and listened to his story an indefinable fear crept over all. We felt awestruck by the nameless and numerous dangers that evidently beset us on every side. Even Cheek's courage sank, and his hitherto buoyant and cheerful spirit was depressed at hearing of the perils of the place. He spoke despondingly and his mind was uneasy, restless, and fearful. "I am afraid," said he, "and I acknowledge it. I never felt fear before but now I feel it." A melancholy that seemed like a presentiment of his own fate possessed him, and to us he was serious almost to sadness until he met his death a few days afterwards from the same Blackfeet from whom Colter escaped.

Colter told us the particulars of a second adventure, which I will give to the reader. In the winter, when he had recovered from the fatigues of his long race and journey, he wished to recover the traps which he had dropped into the Jefferson Fork on the first appearance of the Indians who captured him. He supposed the Indians were all quiet in winter quarters, and retraced his steps to the Gallatin Fork. He had just passed the mountain gap and encamped on the bank of the river for the night and kindled a fire to cook his supper of buffalo meat when he heard the crackling of leaves and branches behind him in the direction of the river. He could see nothing, it being quite dark, but he quickly heard the cocking of guns and instantly leaped over the fire. Several shots followed and bullets whistled around him, knocking the coals off his fire over the ground.

Again he fled for life, and the second time ascended the perpendicular mountain which he had gone up in his former flight, fearing now, as then, that the pass might be guarded by Indians. He reached the top before morning and resting for the day descended the next night, and then made his way with all possible speed to the fort. He said that at the time he promised God Almighty that he would never return to this region again if he were only permitted to escape once more with his life. He did escape once more, and was now again in the same country courting the same dangers which he had so often braved, and that seemed to have for him a kind of fascination. Such men, and there are thousands of them, can only live in a state of excitement and constant action. Perils and danger are their natural element and their familiarity with them, and indifference to their fate, are well illustrated in these adventures of Colter.

A few days afterward, when Cheek was killed

and Colter had another narrow escape, he came into the fort and said he had promised his Maker to leave the country, and "now" said he, throwing down his hat on the ground, "if God will only forgive me this time and let me off I *will* leave the country day after tomorrow, and be d—d if I ever come into it again." He left, accordingly, in company with young Bryant of Philadelphia, whose father was a merchant of that city, and one other whose name I forget. They were attacked by the Blackfeet just beyond the mountains, but escaped by hiding in a thicket, where the Indians were afraid to follow them, and at night they proceeded towards the Big Horn, lying concealed in the daytime. They reached St. Louis safely, and a few years after I heard of Colter's death by jaundice.

We arrived at the Forks of the Missouri on the third day of April, 1810, ten months after leaving St. Louis and two months and one day after quitting my cabin above the Gros Ventre village. We had now reached our place of business, trapping for beaver, and prepared to set to work. Dougherty, Brown, Weir, and myself agreed to trap in company on the Missouri between the Forks and the Falls, which lie several hundred miles down the river to the north from the Forks. We made two canoes by hollowing out the trunks of two trees, and on the third or fourth day after our arrival at the Forks we were ready to start on an expedition down the river.

The rest of the Americans with a few French, in all eighteen in number, determined to go up the Jefferson River for trapping, and the rest of the company under Col. Menard remained to complete the fort and trading house at the Forks between the Jefferson and Madison rivers. On parting from Cheek he said in a melancholy tone: "James, you are going down the Missouri, and it is the general opinion that you will be killed. The Blackfeet are at the Falls, encamped, I hear, and we fear you will never come back. But I am afraid for myself as well as you. I know not the cause, but I have felt fear ever since I came to the Forks, and I never was afraid of anything before. You may come out safe, and I may be killed. Then you will say, there was Cheek afraid to go with us down the river for fear of death, and now he has found his grave by going up the river. I may be dead when you return."

His words made little impression on me at the time, but his tragical end a few days afterwards recalled them to my mind and stamped them on my memory forever. I endeavored to persuade him to join our party, while he was equally urgent for me to join his, saying that if we went in one company our force would afford more protection from Indians than in small parties, while

I contended that the fewer our numbers the better would be our chance of concealment and escape from any war parties that might be traversing the country. We parted, never to meet again, taking opposite directions and both of us going into the midst of dangers. My company of four started down the river and caught some beaver on the first day. On the second we passed a very high spur of the mountain on our right. The mountains in sight on our left were not so high as those to the east of us. On the third day we issued from very high and desolate mountains on both sides of us, whose tops are covered with snow throughout the year, and came upon a scene of beauty and magnificence combined, unequalled by any other view of nature that I ever beheld. It really realized all my conceptions of the Garden of Eden. In the west the peaks and pinnacles of the Rocky Mountains shone resplendent in the sun. The snow on their tops sent back a beautiful reflection of the rays of the morning sun. From the sides of the dividing ridge between the waters of the Missouri and Columbia there sloped gradually down to the bank of the river we were on, a plain, then covered with every variety of wild animals peculiar to this region, while on the east another plain arose by a very gradual ascent and extended as far as the eye could reach. These and the mountain sides were dark with buffaloes, elk, deer, moose, wild goats, and wild sheep; some grazing, some lying down under the trees, and all enjoying a perfect millenium of peace and quiet. On the margin the swans, geese, and pelicans cropped the grass or floated on the surface of the water. The cottonwood trees seemed to have been planted by the hand of man on the bank of the river to shade our way, and the pines and cedars waved their tall, majestic heads along the base and on the sides of the mountains.

The whole landscape was that of the most splendid English park. The stillness, beauty, and loveliness of this scene struck us all with indescribable emotions. We rested on the oars and enjoyed the whole view in silent astonishment and admiration. Nature seemed to have rested here, after creating the wild mountains and chasms among which we had voyaged for two days. Dougherty, as if inspired by the scene with the spirit of poetry and song, broke forth in one of Burns' noblest lyrics, which found a deep echo in our hearts. We floated on till evening through this most delightful country, when we stopped and prepared supper on the bank of the river. We set our traps and before going to rest for the night we examined them and found a beaver in every one, being twenty-three in all. In the morning we were nearly as successful as before, and were cheered with thoughts of making a speedy fortune.

We determined to remain in this second paradise as long as our pursuits would permit. We skinned our beaver, ate breakfast, and started to go farther down the river in search of a good camp ground. Brown and Dougherty started in a canoe before Weir and I were ready, and after going about two hundred yards they struck a rock concealed under the water, overturned the canoe, and lost all our skins and ammunition except the little powder in our horns and the few skins left behind. They also lost their guns, but saved themselves and the canoe. Weir and I soon followed them, and we all encamped at the mouth of a small creek on the left side of the river. Here Weir and I remained while the two others went back to the fort to procure other guns and ammunition, taking with them one of our guns. They reached the fort the first night, having saved a great distance by crossing the country and cutting off the bend of the river, which here makes a large sweep to the east. They went up on the west side, or that next to the mountains, waded Jefferson's Fork and entered the fort late at night.

Early the next morning the whole garrison was aroused by an alarm made by Vallé and several Frenchmen who came in as if pursued by enemies and informed them that the whole party who had gone up the Jefferson at the time of our departure down the Missouri had been killed by the Indians, and that they expected an immediate attack on the fort. The whole garrison prepared for resistance. The next morning after Vallé's arrival Colter came in unhurt, with a few others, and said there were no Indians near the fort. Colonel Menard despatched Dougherty and Brown on the same day to us with the request that we should hasten to the fort to assist in its defense. Being well mounted, they came up to our camp as we were preparing dinner. Their faces were pale with fright, and in great trepidation they told us they had seen Indian *signs* on the route from the fort—that a horse with a rope about his neck had run up and snuffed around them as if in search of his master, and then disappeared—that an Indian dog had performed the same action.

Everything indicated that Indians were near, and we hastened to depart for the fort. We proceeded up the creek near whose mouth we had encamped, and were screened from view on the north by the willows on our right. We had gone very cautiously four miles when we left the river and I perceived a small herd of buffaloes in the creek bottom far to our right start bounding off as if from pursuers in the rear, and immediately after I descried through an opening in the willows eight Indians walking rapidly across the plain in the direction of our late camp. I informed the others of my observation and Weir, horror-stricken, proposed immediate flight. I protested against this course and no one seconded him, but we were all alarmed and the chins and lips of some quivered as they spoke. I said that we could not all escape, having but two horses among us; that we had, perhaps, seen the whole force of the Indians, and that they might not have seen us at all; that we could fight eight with success. I proposed that, if attacked, we should make a breast-work of our horses and two of us should fire upon them at a hundred yards; that the other two should fire at fifty yards; that the reloaded guns should despatch the third couple; and our knives and pistols finish the seventh and eighth.

This Bobadil proposition revived their spirits wonderfully, and they instantly dismissed all thoughts of flight.[35] Weir and I ascended a small height to watch the Indians, while the rest went on with the horses, which travelled slowly with packs. Here we saw the Indians go up to our deserted camp, the smoke from which had attracted them thither. The smoke in this clear atmosphere is visible to a great distance. The hunters said they had seen the smoke from an ordinary fire in the prairies for three hundred miles. We proceeded without pursuit, and at two o'clock the

[35] In Ben Jonson's comedy "Every Man in his Humor," Captain Bobadil is a cowardly adventurer who passes himself off on young and simple observers as a Hector.

next morning we reached the Jefferson Fork, opposite the fort. Unwilling to risk the danger of an attack by delay, we forded the river with great difficulty and went towards the fort, whence some dogs rushed upon us, barking furiously. I spoke to the dogs, and a voice hailed us from the fort with "Who's there"? I answered promptly and thus saved ourselves from a volley, for when we entered the fort the whole garrison was drawn up with fingers upon triggers. They were expecting an attack every moment, and did not look for us so soon. They were all in the greatest consternation. Lieutenant Immell, with those before mentioned of the trapping party up the river, had come in and they supposed that all the rest had been killed.[36] They had had a very narrow escape

[36]"Emmel's Fork," a tributary of the Yellowstone, is shown on Mrs. Carrington's map in *Absaraka*, reprinted as the Lakeside Classics volume for 1950, and this portion of Bridger's route from Fort Laramie to the Montana mines is described on page 293. Another and in some respects clearer depiction of Bridger's route is shown on the map of Montana Territory drawn for the use of the first Legislature in 1865, reproduced in the Society of Montana Pioneers, *Constitution* . . . p. XIII. Lieutenant Michael Immell, for whom the stream was named, served in the First U.S. Infantry from June, 1807 to October, 1808. Resigning his commission, he joined the Upper Missouri expedition of 1809, and for many years thereafter was associated with Manuel Lisa's trading activities. Major Stephen H. Long, leader of the U.S. exploring expedition to the Rocky Mountains in 1819–20, reported that Immell's party was massacred in an encounter with

themselves, as all but Colter probably considered it; he, with his large experience, naturally looked upon the whole as an ordinary occurrence.

During the day others came in and we learned from them the extent of our losses. The company, consisting of eighteen, had proceeded up the bank of the Jefferson, trapping, and on the third day had pitched their tents for the night near the river, and about forty miles from the fort. Cheek, Hull, and Ayers were employed in preparing the camp, while the rest had dispersed in various directions to kill game when some thirty or forty

the Blackfeet. Benjamin O'Fallon, in reporting the affair to General William Clark, stated: "In some respects he was an extraordinary man. He was brave, uncommonly large, and of great muscular strength. When timely apprised of danger, he was a host in himself." H. M. Chittenden, *The American Fur Trade of the Far West*, I, 154.

One further, second-hand, report of Immell's death was recorded by Lieutenant James H. Bradley in 1876. An Indian had told the story some twenty years after the event to Alexander Culbertson of the American Fur Company, who in turn repeated it to Bradley.

Immell's party, the story runs, had ascended the Yellowstone almost to its source, obtaining a large stock of furs. They were followed, however, by a large party of Blood Indians, awaiting an opportunity to surprise the trappers, who killed the entire party, capturing its furs and other supplies. The story became current among the trappers, and either from the remains they found or from some other cause they fixed upon the mouth of this river as the scene of the massacre, and in memory of the leader named it Immell's River. Montana Hist. Soc. *Contributions*, II, 154-55.

Indians appeared on the prairie south of them, running a foot and on horses toward the camp. Vallé and two men whose names I forget came running up to Cheek and others and told them to catch their horses and escape. This Cheek refused to do, but, seizing his rifle and pistols, said he would stay and abide his fate. "My time has come, but I will kill at least two of them, and then I don't care." His gloomy forebodings were about to be fulfilled through his own recklessness and obstinacy. Ayers ran frantically about, paralyzed by fear and crying: "O God, O God, what can I do." Though a horse was within his reach he was disabled by terror from mounting and saving his life. Courage and cowardice met the same fate, though in very different manners. Hull stood coolly examining his rifle as if for battle. The enemy were coming swiftly toward them and Vallé and his two companions started off, pursued by mounted Indians. The sharp reports of Cheek's rifle and pistols were soon heard doing the work of death upon the savages, and then a volley of musketry sent the poor fellow to his long home.

Lieutenant Immell and another came in from hunting about dusk, ignorant of the fate of their fellows, and seeing the tent gone they supposed the place of the camp had been changed. Hearing a noise at the river, Immell went down to the bank, whence he saw through the willows on the opposite side a camp of thirty Indian lodges, a woman coming down to the river with a brass kettle which he would have sworn was his own, and also a white man bound by both arms to a tree. He could not recognize the prisoner, but supposed he was an American. On returning to the place where Cheek had pitched his tent, he saw his dead body without the scalp, lying where he had bravely met his end. He then hastened to the fort, where his arrival has been noticed before.

A greater part of the garrison, with myself, started out on the morning of my coming in to go in pursuit of the Indians up the river, and to bury our dead. We found and buried the corpses of our murdered comrades, Cheek and Ayers, the latter being found in the river near the bank. Hull was never heard of, and two others, Rucker and Fleehart, were also missing, being killed or taken prisoners by the Indians. An Indian was found dead with two bullets in his body, supposed to be from Cheek's pistol. The body was carefully concealed under leaves and earth and surrounded by logs. We followed the trail of the savages for two days, when we missed it and gave up the chase. Many of the men wished to pursue them into the mountains, but Colonel Menard judged it imprudent to go farther in search of them, as we should probably come upon an army, of which this party was but a detachment. He thought the main body was very large and not distant from us or the fort, and therefore determined to return and await them there. We accordingly retraced our steps to the fort and remained in it with our whole force for several days, expecting an attack.

No attack was made, however, nor did an enemy make his appearance afterwards, except in the shape of white, grey, brown, and grizzly bears. Seeing nothing of our enemies, the Blackfeet, we soon became emboldened and ventured out of the fort to hunt and trap, to the distance of about six miles. In these short expeditions the men had frequent encounters with bears, which in this region are of enormous size, sometimes weighing 800 pounds each, and when wounded are the most terribly ferocious and dangerous to the hunter of all other animals. The African lion and Bengal tiger are the only beasts of prey that in ferocity and power can be compared with the grey or grizzly bear of the Rocky Mountains. These were the terrors of our men as much as were the Indians, and they usually spoke of them both as equally terrible and equally to be avoided. The great strength of the bear, his swiftness and utter insensibility to danger when wounded, render him as dangerous to the hunter as the lion or the tiger. The first shot is seldom fatal upon him, on account of the thickness of his skin and skull and the great quantity of fat and flesh that envelope his heart and make an almost impenetrable shield in front. I will relate a few adventures with this North American king of beasts, and then proceed with my narrative.[37]

Weir, an American, was hunting on an island in the Madison River a short distance from the fort and came suddenly, in a buffalo path, upon a white or grey bear. He fired at the monster, wounded him in the breast, and then ran for his life with the bear at his heels and saved himself by plunging into the river. His pursuer laid himself down on the bank and in the last struggle of death fell into the water, where he died. Weir drew him out, took off the skin, and was cutting and hanging up the meat when he heard the noise of another bear in the thicket near by. He hastened to the fort for assistance and a party, with me, went over to the island. When there, we sep-

[37]Lewis and Clark first encountered the grizzly bear in Montreal County in western North Dakota in the spring of 1805. At this time the explorers were anxious to encounter them, having seen an abundance of their tracks. Before many weeks their "anxiety" was more than satisfied and they were quite content to leave the grizzlies alone, if only the latter would return the favor. Lewis, even more emphatic than James, recorded that he would rather encounter two Indians than one grizzly. The modern high power rifle long since turned the balance against the grizzly and in favor of the hunter. Despite this advantage, shocking tales of sorry experiences with grizzlies are still occasionally told.

arated in our search and in beating about the bushes I, with my dog, entered a narrow path and had gone some distance when I saw the dog ahead suddenly bristle up, bark, and walk lightly as if scenting danger. I called to the men to come up, and watched the dog. He soon found the bear guarding a dead elk, which he and his dead companion had killed and covered with leaves. As soon as he saw the dog he plunged at him and came furiously toward me, driving the dog before him and snorting and raging like a mad bull. I leveled my gun and snapped and then ran, with the bear at my heels and his hot breath upon me. I reached the river bank and turned short up a path, in which I met my companions coming to my call. They, however, seeing me running, were panic stricken and took to their heels also. Thus were we all in full retreat from Bruin, who crossed the river and fled through the willows on the other side. We heard him crashing his way for many hundred yards.

On another occasion a party had wounded a bear, which instantly gave chase and overtook a Shawnee Indian in the company, named Luthe-caw, who had stumbled over some brush and fallen. He grasped the Indian by the double *ca-pote* and coat collar and stood over him, while we fired six shots into the bear, which fell dead upon the Indian, who cried out that the bear was crushing him to death, but arose unhurt as soon as we removed the tremendous weight of the dead monster from his body. His jaws were firmly closed upon the Shawnee's capeau and coat collar, who arose at last with *"sacre moste, l'est crazy monte"*—"damn the bear, he almost mashed me."

We kept the flag flying a month, frequently seeing Indians without getting an interview with them, they always fleeing at our approach. We then pulled down the flag and hoisted the scalp of the Indian whom Cheek had killed. By this time the fort was completed and put in a good state of defense. We subsisted ourselves in the meantime by hunting in small parties which started out of the fort before day and went some twenty or thirty miles, and after having killed a buffalo or elk came back with the meat loaded on the horses.

The grizzly bears frequently made their appearance and we killed great numbers of them. A Yankee, named Pelton, was remarkable for his contracted, narrow eyes, which resembled those of a bear. He was a jovial, popular fellow, and had greatly amused the company in coming up the river by his songs and sermons. At every stopping place he held a meeting for the mock trial of offenders and exhorted us in the New England style to mend our courses and eschew sin. He had an adventure with a bear about this time

which is worth relating. While trapping near the
fort with a small party, including myself, he was
watching his traps alone, a short distance from
us, when he heard a rustling in the bushes at his
right, and before turning around he was attacked
by a large bear, which grasped him by the breast,
bore him to the earth, and stood over him with his
head back and eyes fixed on his face as if observing his features. Pelton screamed and yelled in a
most unearthly manner, and his new acquaintance, as if frightened by his appearance and
voice, leaped from over his body, stood and looked
at him a moment over his shoulder, growled,
and then walked off. We ran in the direction of
the cries and soon met Pelton coming towards us
in a walk, grumbling and cursing, with his head
down as if he had been disturbed in a comfortable
sleep, and altogether wearing an air of great dissatisfaction. He told us the story, and thought he
owed his escape to his bearish eyes which discon-
certed his friendly relation in the act of making a
dinner of him.[38]

[38]The waggish Pelton met a sorry fate. In the late summer of 1811 the overland Astorian party of Wilson P.
Hunt and Donald McKenzie encountered among the
friendly Snakes on the Lewis River a young American
"who was deranged but who sometimes recovered his
reason." In his lucid intervals he stated that he was
Archibald Pelton, a native of Connecticut, who had ascended the Missouri as a member of Andrew Henry's
party, all of whom had been massacred except himself

The Indians, we thought, kept the game away from the vicinity of the fort. Thus we passed the time till the month of May, when a party of twenty-one, of whom I was one, determined to go up the Jefferson River to trap. By keeping together we hoped to repel any attack of the sav-

about three years before. Escaping, unperceived, from the attackers, he had wandered about for some weeks until he fell in with the friendly tribe in whose company the Astorians found him. In the hope that contact with white people would restore his reason, McKenzie conducted him on to Astoria, where record of his further career ceases.

Such was Pelton's own story, obviously incorrect in several important particulars. When the trappers became discouraged (as James relates) over the incessant attacks of the Blackfeet, one group (in which James was numbered) returned to St. Louis. Another party, led by Henry, crossed the Rockies from the headwaters of the Yellowstone to those of the Columbia, hoping thus to escape their tormenters and continue their trapping operations. The party passed the winter of 1810–11 in a fort on the branch of Snake River which is still called Henry's Fork. Although the natives proved friendly they were poverty-stricken, and after undergoing severe privations the party returned to St. Louis in the summer of 1811.

How Pelton became separated from his companions must forever remain a mystery. His story of the massacre suggests that in his befuddled state he was trying to tell of the hostilities between the Blackfeet and the trappers. Instead of three years, his sojourn among the Snakes could hardly have lasted more than a few months at most. For his story see Ross Cox, *Adventures on the Columbia River* (New York, 1832), 60–61; Gabriel Franchère, *Narrative of a Voyage to the Northwest Coast of North America* .. ., in Thwaites (Ed.), *Early Western Travels*, VI, 271.

ages. We soon found the trapping in such numbers not very profitable, and changed our plan by separating in companies of four, of whom two men would trap while two watched the camp. In this manner we were engaged until the fear of Indians began to wear off and we all became more venturous.

One of our company, a Shawnee half-breed named Druyer, the principal hunter of Lewis and Clark's party, went up the river one day and set his traps about a mile from the camp. In the morning he returned alone and brought back six beavers. I warned him of his danger. "I am too much of an Indian to be caught by Indians," said he. On the next day he repeated the adventure and returned with the product of his traps, saying: "This is the way to catch beaver." On the third morning he started again up the river to examine his traps, when we advised him to wait for the whole party, which was about moving farther up the stream, and at the same time two other Shawnees left us, against our advice, to kill deer.

We started forward in company and soon found the dead bodies of the last mentioned hunters, pierced with lances, arrows, and bullets and lying near each other. Farther on, about one hundred and fifty yards, Druyer and his horse lay dead, the former mangled in a horrible manner; his head was cut off, his entrails torn out, and his body hacked to pieces. We saw from the marks on the ground that he must have fought in a circle on horseback and probably killed some of his enemies, being a brave man and well armed with a rifle, pistol, knife, and tomahawk. We pursued the trail of the Indians till night without overtaking them, and then returned, having buried our dead, with saddened hearts to the fort.[39]

[39]George Drouillard was regarded by Lewis and Clark as one of the most valuable members of their exploring expedition. Following its conclusion, he returned to the Upper Missouri in the employ of Manuel Lisa, and in 1810 met his death in the manner our author relates. Drouillard's father was Pierre Drouillard of Detroit, where the family has now resided for over two hundred years. Pierre was for many years an official of the British Indian Department at Detroit and during the Revolutionary period was, of course, an enemy of the Americans, This fact negatives the statement sometimes made that he was a Kentuckian and a friend of George Rogers Clark. He was born on Isle Orleans below Quebec in 1744 and was buried at Detroit, April 16, 1803.

Pierre married Angelica Descomps *dit* Labadie on Nov. 20, 1776 and children were born to the couple at Detroit in 1778, 1780, 1781, 1783, 1784, and 1786. Prior to the union with his white wife Drouillard had cohabited with an Indian woman and a child (named Pierre) of their union was baptized at Assumption Church in Sandwich (opposite Detroit), Sept. 27, 1775. George Drouillard was also the son of Pierre and an Indian woman. Since Pierre served as interpreter to the Huron, it seems probable that the mother belonged to this tribe.

In 1929 Miss Gertie Drouillard of Windsor brought to

Soon after this time Marie and St. John, my
two Canadian companions on the route from my
winter quarters on the Missouri to the Big Horn,
came to the fort at the Forks. Marie's right eye
was out and he carried the yet fresh marks of a
horrible wound on his head and under his jaw.
After I had left them at the Big Horn to come to
the Forks, they came on to the Twenty-five Yard
River, the most western branch of the Yellowstone, for the purpose of trapping.[40] One morn-

the Detroit Public Library a letter written by George
Drouillard from St. Louis, May 23, 1809 to his half-sister,
Marie Louise Parent (*nee* Drouillard) at Detroit. In it the
writer bewails the trouble he had encountered over the
shooting of a deserter in the Upper Country at the behest,
as he states, of Manuel Lisa (their employer). But for this,
and the subsequent trial at St. Louis he would have visited his Detroit home. The letter breathes the utmost
affection for his family, including "all my brothers and
sisters" and "our mama, whom I embrace" Evidently
this refers to Pierre Drouillard's white wife, and not to
George's Indian mother. The entire context strongly implies that he had been reared as a member of the Pierre
Drouillard family. Compelled by lack of means to depart
upon another three-year engagement on the Upper Missouri, as a member of the St. Louis Missouri Fur Company expedition in which James also enlisted, the writer
promises to pay his Detroit relatives a visit as soon as he
returns, "all of whom I wish very much to see."

[40]Twenty-five Yard River, otherwise known as Shields
River, enters the Yellowstone from the north in present-
day Park County, a few miles below Livingston, Montana.
At this point the northward-flowing Yellowstone turns
sharply eastward. John Shields, for whom the river is
named, was a member of the Lewis and Clark expedition.

ing, after setting his traps, Marie strolled out into the prairie for game and soon perceived a large white bear rolling on the ground in the shade of a tree. Marie fired at and missed him. The bear snuffed around him without rising, and did not see the hunter until he had re-loaded, fired again, and wounded him. His Majesty instantly, with ears set back, flew towards his enemy like an arrow, who ran for his life, reached a beaver dam across the river, and seeing no escape by land, plunged into the water above the dam. The bear followed and soon proved himself as much superior to his adversary in swimming as in running. Marie dove and swam under the

Oddly enough, Clark named another stream for him, Highwood Creek, which enters the Missouri from the south about midway between Fort Benton and Great Falls. Shields River is scarcely large enough to be termed a "branch" of the Yellowstone. Of it Lieutenant James H. Bradley wrote in 1876: "Shield's river received its name from Captain Clark in 1806, in honor of one of his men. The trappers of early times have called it Twenty-five Yard Creek, and it was a famous resort for them, abounding as it did with innumerable beaver. Two reasons are assigned for the name; its width, which *isn't* twenty-five yards, but much less [but note that Captain Clark in 1806 described it as 35 yards wide]: and the asserted fact that it rises only twenty-five yards from the source of another stream, which I can neither affirm nor deny. Many sharp conflicts occurred here in olden times between the resolute trapper bands that were wont to frequent this locality and the vengeful Blackfeet who then lorded over it." Montana Historical Soc., *Contributions*, II, 152.

water as long as he could, when he rose to the surface near the bear. He saved himself by diving and swimming in this manner several times, but his enemy followed close upon him and watched his motions with the sagacity which distinguishes these animals. At last he came up from under the water directly beneath the jaws of the monster, which seized him by the head, the tushes piercing the scalp and neck under the right jaw and crushing the ball of his right eye. In this situation, with his head in the bear's mouth and he swimming with him ashore, St. John, having heard his two shots in quick succession, came running to his rescue. St. John levelled his rifle and shot the bear in the head, and then dragged out Marie from the water, more dead than alive. I saw him six days afterwards, with a swelling on his head an inch thick, and his food and drink gushed through the opening under his jaw made by the teeth of his terrible enemy.

We made frequent hunting excursions in small parties, in which nothing of consequence occurred. Many of us had narrow escapes from Indians and still narrower from the grizzly and white bears. Game became very scarce, and our enemies seemed bent upon starving us out. We all became tired of this kind of life, cooped up in a small enclosure and in perpetual danger of assassination when outside the pickets. The

Blackfeet manifested so determined a hatred and jealousy of our presence that we could entertain no hope of successfully prosecuting our business, even if we could save our lives, in their country. Discouraged by the prospect before us, most of the Americans prepared to go back to the settlements, while Colonel Henry and the greater part of the company, with a few Americans, were getting ready to cross the mountains and go onto the Columbia beyond the vicinity of our enemies.

A party which had been left at Manuel's fort for the purpose had brought up one of the boats and part of the goods from the *cache* on the Yellowstone below the fort, as far as Clark's River, where, on account of the rapidity of the current, they had been compelled to leave them. Thither Menard went with men and horses to get the goods for the trip to the Columbia, and I accompanied him, with most of the Americans, on our way back to civilized life and the enjoyments of home. When we reached the Twenty-five Yard River we met one hundred and fifty Indians of the Gros Ventre tribe. One of the men, observing a new calico shirt belonging to him around the neck of an Indian, informed Menard of his suspicions that this party had robbed the *cache* (from the French, *cacher* to hide) of the goods which they had hidden in the earth near the bank of the

Yellowstone, in the fall before.[41] Menard questioned them, but they denied the theft, saying they got the calico at the trading house. In the evening they entrenched themselves behind breastworks of logs and brush, as if fearing an attack from us, and in the morning departed on an expedition against the Snakes, of which miserable nation, we heard afterwards, they killed and took for slaves a large number. Thus the whales of this wilderness destroy the minnows.

Here we made three canoes of buffalo bull's skins by sewing together two skins for each canoe and then stretching them over a frame similar in shape to a Mackinaw boat. Our canoe contained three men, about sixty steel traps, five hundred

[41]The Indian practice of concealing food supplies and other goods in holes made in the ground for preservation for future use was noted by the earliest white visitors to the interior of the continent. So useful was the custom that it was soon adopted by the white explorers and traders, and numerous descriptions of it are scattered through the several Lakeside Classics volumes. Zenas Leonard's narrative, the Classics volume for 1934, pp. 258–59, provides one interesting account of the construction of caches by white trappers in 1835. Others are given by Josiah Gregg, *The Commerce of the Prairies* (the Classics volume for 1926, pp. 56–58); *Kit Carson's Autobiography* (the Classics volume for 1935, pp. 28–29); Alexander Ross, *Adventures of the First Settlers on the Oregon or Columbia River* (the Classics volume for 1923, p. 196); and General Philippe De Frobriand, *Army Life in Dakota* (the Classics volume for 1941, pp. 131–32).

beaver skins, our guns and ammunition, besides other commodities. Nine of us started down the river in these canoes and in two days reached Clark's River, where the boat with the goods was awaiting us. The rest went with the horses by land. Clark's River enters the Yellowstone from the south. Near its mouth we found an army of the Crow nation encamped.[42] This is a wandering tribe, like most of the Indians in this region, without any fixed habitation. These were then at war with the Blackfeet, whom they were seeking to give battle. Having remained with us a few days, they went off towards the south.

One of our hunters came into camp on the evening of the day when they had departed and informed us of a large force of Indians about four miles to the north, stationed behind a breast-work of rocks and earth near a cliff. These were supposed to be Blackfeet, and early in the morning, the land party with the horses having arrived, we mustered our whole force and went out to attack them in their entrenchment. We were all eager for the fight, and advancing upon them in Indian style we discovered instead of Blackfeet about a hundred warriors of the Crow nation, who had

[42]Clark's River is shown on some modern maps as Clark's Creek. It rises in Yellowstone Park and after flowing eastward some distance turns northward across Carbon County, Montana, entering the Yellowstone a few miles below the village of Park City.

been out on an expedition against the Blackfeet and had just returned. They were a detachment from the army which had left us the day before. They marched into our camp on horseback, two abreast, and there learning from us the news of their comrades, they immediately crossed the river in pursuit of them.

Their manner of crossing the river was singular, and reminded me of the roving Tartars. They stripped themselves entirely naked and every ten piled their accouterments together, blankets, saddles, weapons, &c. on a tent skin made of buffalo robes, and tying it up in a large round bundle threw it into the river and plunged after it, some swimming with these huge heaps, floating like corks, and others riding the horses or holding by the tails till they had all crossed the river. Arrived on the opposite bank, which they reached in little less time than I have taken to describe their passage, they dressed, mounted their horses, and marched off two and two as before, and were quickly out of our sight.

Here we parted from our companions who were going to the Columbia, and who returned hence to the Forks with the goods and ammunition for their trip, while we, the homeward bound, continued our course down the river in the canoes and the boat they had left to the fort on the Big Horn. We remained here several days, repairing a keel boat left by Manuel two years before, which we loaded with the goods from the canoes, and then recommenced our descent of the Yellowstone with the canoes and two boats. Colonel Menard accompanied us in one of the boats, and I with two companions kept to our canoe in advance of the others for the purpose of killing game.

On reaching the place of *cacheing* the goods and leaving the boats on account of the ice the year before, Menard verified his suspicions of the Gros Ventres whom we met on the Twenty-five Yard River. The pit containing the goods and effects of the men had been opened and forty trunks robbed of their contents. Another pit, containing the Company's goods, had also been opened, and the most valuable of its store left by Menard had been taken off by the Gros Ventres. They had also cut up and nearly destroyed the boats. We repaired one with the fragments of the other and then passed down the river with three boats. I kept ahead, as before, in my skin canoe.

This river is very rapid throughout its whole course, and very shallow. We were now near the Falls, which are difficult and dangerous of navigation. In the morning I killed two buffaloes with my pistol and rifle, and my two companions killed two more, which we cut up and stowed away. We approached the Falls sooner than we expected, and were directing our course to the left side among the sunken rocks and breakers, where we would certainly have been lost, when we heard a gun behind us and saw the men on the boats waving us with handkerchiefs to the right.[43] We were barely able to gain the channel, when the canoe shot down the descent with wonderful rapidity. We flew along the water like a sledge down an icy hill. My two companions lay in the bottom of the canoe, which frequently rebounded from the waves made by the rocks under the water and stood nearly upright. The waves washed over us and nearly filled the canoe with water.

[43]The Bad Lands of the Yellowstone extend from the mouth of the Tongue River at Miles City to Glendive. Throughout this area the river's course is marked by a series of rapids. Our earliest account of them is the one left by Captain Clark, who descended this portion of the Yellowstone July 30–31, 1806. The first of these, about a dozen miles below Miles City, Clark named Buffalo Shoals "from the circumstance of one of these animals being in them." The name is still retained on modern maps. Clark's party felt compelled to let the canoes down by hand for fear of being destroyed by striking upon submerged rocks. He characterized the rapid as "by far the worst place" he had seen on the river from the Rocky Mountains downward, a distance, by his calculation of 694 miles. James, like Clark in 1806, was passing hurriedly down the river and his account of the descent is extremely sketchy. His spirited description of the "Falls" evidently applies to the Buffalo Rapid or Shoal.

The boats behind commenced the descent soon after we had ended it in safety. They several times struck, and one of them hung fast on a concealed rock. We hauled our canoe ashore, carried it above, and coming down to the foundered boat and lighting it of part of its load, we got it off the rocks. We now passed rapidly down to the Missouri River, where I left my friendly canoe and went aboard one of the boats. Here my spirits were cheered with the near prospect of home. I longed to see the familiar faces of kindred and friends with a yearning of the heart which few can realize who have not wandered, as I had done, among savages and wild beasts and made the earth my bed and the sky my canopy for more than a year. My way homeward was clear and comparatively safe; the tribes along the river being friendly or, if hostile, unable to annoy us as the Blackfeet had done so long in the prairies.

In my wanderings on this expedition I saw much of the Indians and their manner of living. Those in this region were then more savage, less degraded, and more virtuous than they are at the present time. The white man and his fire water have sadly demoralized them, thinned their numbers, and will soon sink them into oblivion. They are no longer the proud, haughty, simple minded warriors and orators that I found so many of them to be in 1809-'10. Sunk in poverty and intemperance, they are fast dwindling away. I have seen some of the finest specimens of men among our North American Indians. I have seen chiefs with the dignity of real princes and the eloquence of real orators, and braves with the valor of the ancient Spartans. Their manner of speaking is extremely dignified and energetic. They gesticulate with infinite grace, freedom, and animation. Their words flow deliberately, conveying their ideas with great force and vividness of expression deep into the hearts of their hearers. Among their speakers I recognized all the essentials in manner of consummate orators. I shall have occasion in the following chapters to bring out some of their nobler qualities in bolder relief than was possible in the preceding, on account of the more intimate relations I afterwards formed with these children of nature and the prairies.

In five days after entering the Missouri we descended to the Gros Ventre village and our fort, and were there joyfully received by our old companions. Whiskey flowed like milk and honey in the land of Canaan, being sold to the men by the disinterested and benevolent gentlemen of the Missouri Fur Company for the moderate sum of twelve dollars per gallon, they taking in payment beaver skins at one dollar and a half each,

which were worth in St. Louis, six. Their prices
for every thing else were in about the same proportion. Even at this price some of the men
bought whiskey by the bucket full and drank

> " 'Till they forgot their loves and debts
> And cared for grief na mair."

During the carousal an incident occurred that
nearly brought ruin upon us all. Three Shawnee
Indians in the company from Kaskaskia had
started from the Upper Yellowstone in a skin
canoe in advance, and had arrived a day or two
before us. On their way down, one of them,
named Placota, had wantonly killed a Crow Indian on the Yellowstone and a Gros Ventre on
the Missouri, about sixty miles above the village,
and taken their scalps. In his drunken fit Placota
brought out one of these scalps in full view of
the friendly Gros Ventres. Menard caught it out
of his hand and hid it from view. The Indians
became greatly excited, crowded around us, and
demanded to know whose scalp it was. Menard
then produced to them the scalp of the Indian
whom Cheek had killed, and which they had
seen before. They said this was a "dry" and the
other a "green" scalp. We at last and with great
difficulty pacified them and quieted their suspicions. Placota, who was raging mad, by Menard's
orders was tied behind the trading house till he

became sober, when I released him on his promise of good behavior.

This tribe was then very powerful, having in all five villages and mustering, in case of emergency, as many as three thousand warriors. I have already noticed their character and warlike qualities. A singular custom prevails among them of cutting off a finger or inflicting a severe wound in remembrance of any severe misfortune. Few of the men thirty years of age were without the marks of these wounds, made on the death of some near relation or on occasion of a defeat of the nation in war. Some I saw with three and one with four fingers cut off. I saw a young man bewailing the death of his father in a battle with the Blackfeet. He had compelled his friends to draw leather cords through the flesh under his arms and on his back, and attaching three buffalo skulls, weighing at least twenty-five pounds, to the ends of the cords he dragged them over the ground after him through the village, moaning and lamenting in great distress.

At their meals, the Indians on the Missouri throw the first piece of meat in the direction of an absent friend. In smoking, they send the first whiff upwards in honor of the Great Spirit, the second downward as a tribute to their great mother, the third to the right and the fourth to the left, in thanks to the Great Spirit for the game he sends them so abundantly on the bosom of the earth. Their name for chief is *Inca*, the same as that of the South American and Mexican Indians. For knife they say *messa*; for horses, *cowalla*. A comparison of their languages will show an identity in their origin and race. They secure their dead by setting four poles, forked at the top and about twenty-five feet in height, in the ground. On these they put a scaffold of buffalo skin, fastened to the poles, and on this the corpse is placed, covered by a buffalo skin bound around it very tightly. In this way the corpse is protected from the birds and beasts, and thus it remains till the scaffold falls by decay. The bones are then gathered by the relatives and put into a common heap. I saw in the rear of the Gros Ventre village an immense extent of ground covered by these tombs in the air, and near by was a heap of skulls and bones which had fallen to the earth from these air graves.

After a few day's stay at the fort and village we again started down the river with Colonel Menard and two boats. We arrived at St. Louis in the month of August, 1810, without any occurrence of interest on the voyage. We never got our dues or anything of the least similitude to justice from the Company. They brought me in their debt two hundred dollars, and some of the other Americans for still larger sums. The reader may ask how this could be. He can easily imagine the process when he is told that the Company charged us six dollars per pound for powder, three dollars for lead, six dollars for coarse calico shirts, one dollar and a half per yard for coarse tow linen for tents, the same for a common butcher knife, and so on, and allowed us only what I have mentioned for our beaver skins, our only means of payment.

Captain Lewis told me not to lay in any supplies in St. Louis as the Company had plenty and would sell them to me as cheaply as I could get them in St. Louis, or nearly so, allowing only for a reasonable profit. Lewis did not intend to deceive us, and was chagrined at the villainous conduct of the Company afterwards. This, with the fraudulent violation of their contracts and promises in the Indian country by this concern makes up a piece of extortion, fraud, and swindling that ought to consign the parties engaged in it to eternal infamy. The heaviest blame must rest on the unprincipled Lisa; but the rest of the Company must suffer the stigma of having connived at and profited by the villainy, if they did not actually originate and urge it onward. I sued them on my contract, and was the only one who did so. After many delays and continuances from term to term I was glad to get rid of the suits and them by giving my note for one hundred dollars to the Company.[44] This, with my debt to Colter, made me a loser to the amount of three hundred dollars by one year's trapping on the headwaters of the Missouri. Some of the Americans, however, fared much worse, and were deterred from returning to the settlements at all by their debts to the Company, which they were hopeless of discharging by any ordinary business in which they could engage. Such is one instance of the kind and considerate justice of wealth to defenseless poverty, beautifully illustrating the truth of the sentiment uttered by somebody, "take care of the rich and the rich will take care of the poor."

[44]Douglas, in a footnote at this point, relates the outcome of James' several suits. In September, 1810 William Clark acting as agent for the Fur Company, sued James on a note for $249.81. James countered with a suit against the Company for breach of contract, claiming damages of $750. After various continuances, both suits were dismissed, apparently by reason of the absence of witnesses. In October, 1814 the Company again sued James on his note, with no judgment shown on the records. In October, 1814 Colter's administrator sued James on a note for $140 given by James to Colter, Oct. 7, 1809. The case was settled without a trial.

CHAPTER III

Adventure to Santa Fe

AFTER my return from the Upper Missouri I went in the fall of 1810 to Pennsylvania, where I remained two years and married. I returned to St. Louis in the fall of 1813, procured a keel boat, and with it navigated the Ohio and Mississippi between Pittsburgh and St. Louis, carrying goods for large profits. I continued in this business till the fall of 1815, when I took a stock of goods from McKnight & Brady[45] of St. Louis and opened a store in Harrisonville,[46]

[45]John McKnight was a Virginian who with his partner, Thomas Brady, arrived at St. Louis with a keel boat cargo of merchandise. They became extensive holders of land at East St. Louis, Harrisonville, and elsewhere. John McKnight never married, but his parents, who with six daughters and five sons settled in St. Louis, generously endowed the town with McKnights. Robert McKnight, who figures in the early Santa Fe trade, was one of John's numerous brothers. Thomas Brady died near St. Louis, Oct. 11, 1821.

[46]Harrisonville was a village in the American Bottom, about thirty miles south of St. Louis, in Monroe County, Illinois. Prior to 1825 it was the seat of government of Monroe County. Although a mere hamlet, it was a shipping point for the interior country. The lack of railroads and the recurrence of floods prevented the town from growing. In 1916, according to Douglas, its population was about 150. At the present time (1953) it consists of a dozen or more houses and one general store.

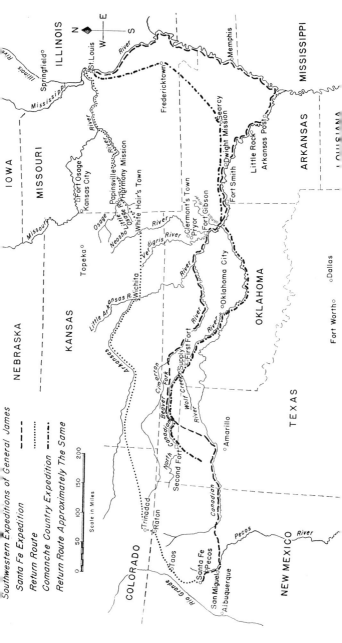

Southwestern Expeditions of General James

Santa Fe Expedition — — —

Return Route ··········

Comanche Country Expedition —··—··—

Return Route Approximately The Same —··—··—

Scale in Miles

0   50   100   150   200

Illinois, dividing profits equally among us. In the fall of 1818 I went to Baltimore with letters of recommendation and bought goods for cash and on credit to the amount of seventeen thousand dollars and brought them in wagons to Pittsburgh, where I left them to await a rise of the river, which was too low for navigation, and came to St. Louis. My goods were not sent on till the following spring, when they had fallen greatly in price and the market was filled with a large supply. I was unable to dispose of my stock even at cost.

I struggled on through the years 1819–20 with the certain prospect of bankruptcy before my face, amid the clamors of creditors, and without the hope of extricating myself from impending ruin. About this time Baum, Baird, and Chambers, with some others, came to St. Louis from Santa Fe, where they had been imprisoned by the Government ever since the year 1810.[47] They, with Rob-

[47] James' brief sketch of the early trade with Santa Fe is considerably inadequate. For further information upon it see I. J. Cox's *"Opening of the Santa Fe Trail"* in *Missouri Hist. Rev.,* XXV, 30–66; Thomas M. Marshall's "St. Vrain's Expedition to the Gila in 1826" in *Southwestern Hist. Quarterly,* XIX, 251–60; and Archer B. Hulbert, *Southwest on the Turquoise Trail* (Denver, 1933). James Baird was a native of Carlisle, Pennsylvania, who removed from Pittsburgh to St. Louis in 1810, where he started a blacksmith shop. His disastrous venture to Santa Fe, in association with William Chambers, Robert McKnight, Peter Baum, and others was undertaken in 1812 instead of 1810, as stated by James. Apparently it was directly

ert, brother of John McKnight of the firm of Mc-
Knight and Brady, and eight others were the first
American Santa Fe traders that carried goods from
St. Louis to New Mexico. Immediately on reaching Santa Fe their goods were confiscated by the
Governor, sold at public auction, and themselves
taken to Chihuahua and there thrown into prison,
where they were kept in more or less strict con-
finement for the space of ten years, being supported during that time by the proceeds of Mc-

inspired by Lieutenant Zebulon M. Pike's report of his
1806–1807 expedition, which was issued as the Lakeside
Classics volume for 1925. In 1822, despite their nine-year
imprisonment in consequence of their first visit to Santa
Fe, Baird and Chambers organized a second expedition.
It started from St. Louis in the autumn, and in consequence was compelled to winter at the crossing of the
Arkansas, eventually continuing on to Chihuahua. About
this time, apparently, Baird decided to throw in his lot
with the Mexicans. In October, 1826, then at El Paso, he
indited a long complaint to the President of the El Paso
District against the operations of Cerain St. Vrain's party
of American fur hunters. In it he stated that he had resided fourteen years in Mexico, conveniently omitting
that nine of them had been passed as a prisoner, and had
acquired Mexican citizenship. Now, as a citizen of the
"Great Mexican Nation" he was revolted by the spectacle
of the lawless American "foreigners" who were despoiling
the country of its natural wealth, and urged that the regulations prescribed by the Government be strictly enforced,
to the end that "we Mexicans may peacefully profit by the
goods with which the merciful God has been pleased to
enrich our soil." By his conduct Baird provided an affirmative answer to the ancient question whether the Ethio-
pian can change his skin or the leopard his spots.

Knight's goods, the Government allowing 18¾ cents per day to each man.

This, I believe, was the second company of Americans that ever entered Santa Fe. Clem. Morgan, a Portuguese and very wealthy, made his way thither at a very early day, while Louisiana belonged to Spain, and returned in safety, making a good venture.[48] General Zebulon Pike was the first American visitor to that country. He went in the year 1806, and on his arrival was marched

[48] "Clem Morgan" was Jacques Clamorgan, one of the most enterprising St. Louis traders of his time. A good deal of mystery still shrouds his career, for which Douglas, editor of the 1916 edition of James' narrative (pp. 293–94), suggests two explanations: the fact that he was of alien blood from the French and Spanish inhabitants of St. Louis; and the further fact that his way of life may have scandalized them, since he maintained a harem of negro or mulatto slave women, whom he emancipated when they bore him children.

Although Clamorgan may have been part Portuguese, his name is clearly Welsh. He came to St. Louis by way of New Orleans in 1784, and died there, aged about eighty, in November, 1814. He obtained extensive grants of land from the Spanish government. He played the leading role in the organization of the Missouri Company in 1794 for trading on the Upper Missouri, and in 1807, past seventy years of age, he headed an expedition to Santa Fe, the first successful one ever sent from Missouri. Data brought to light in comparatively recent years add considerably to our knowledge of the exploring and trading activities of Clamorgan and his Spanish associates. See A. P. Nasatir, "The Formation of the Missouri Company" in *Mo. Hist. Rev.*, XXV, 10–22; A. P. Nasatir, "John Evans, Explorer and Surveyor," *Idem,* XXV, 432–60; A. P. Nasatir,

through Mexico as a prisoner of war, but was soon after released on demand of our Government. One of his men was detained thirteen years by the Spaniards, and returned with Chambers to St. Louis. Pike, in the beginning of our last war with England, met a soldier's death at Queenston Heights.[49] The second company from the United States was McKnight's and their treatment has been noticed. The third was under the command of Auguste Chouteau and DeMun of St. Louis, and was composed entirely of French. They made a very unsuccessful venture, being deprived of their goods worth $40,000, without the least remuneration, and themselves imprisoned for a short time.[50]

"Jacques Clamorgan; Colonial Promoter of the Northern Border of New Spain" in *New Mexico Hist. Rev.*, XVII, 101–12; and David Williams, "John Evans' Strange Journey," in *Am. Hist. Rev.*, LIX, 508–29.

[49]Pike was killed at the storming of York (now Toronto), April 27, 1813.

[50]A detailed account of this expedition is contained in an extensive letter written by De Mun to Governor William Clark, November 25, 1817, which is printed in *American State Papers; Foreign Affairs*, IV, 211–13. Jules de Mun was born of French parentage in San Domingo, April 25, 1782 and after experiencing a variety of vicissitudes came with his mother to Ste. Genevieve in 1808. The expedition with Chouteau was undertaken in the autumn of 1815. Save for an eleven-year absence in Cuba (1819–30) De Mun remained a resident of St. Louis until his death, August 15, 1843, serving in later years as Register of the U. S. Land Office and (subsequently) as Recorder of Deeds. Data adapted from sketch by Douglas, pp. 294–95.

I commanded the fourth expedition to Santa Fe from the United States, and the first that was made after the Mexican Revolution and the declaration of their independence from Spain, and I was the first American that ever visited the country and escaped a prison while there. John McKnight desired to go to Mexico to see his brother, procure his release if he were still in prison, and return with him to the States. The first information he had received concerning Robert in ten years came by his companions above named, who had left him in the interior of Mexico. He proposed that I should take my goods and accompany him, and supposed that under Spanish protection we could go unmolested by the Government. The news of the Revolution had not yet reached this country. This appeared to be the best course to retrieve my affairs, and I prepared for the journey by procuring a passport from Don Luis de Onis, the Spanish Minister, countersigned by John Q. Adams, then Secretary of State under Monroe.

I loaded a keel-boat with goods to the value of $10,000 and laid in a large quantity of biscuit, whiskey, flour, lead, and powder for trading with the Indians on the route. I started from St. Louis on the tenth of May, 1821, and descended the Mississippi to the mouth of the Arkansas. The company consisted, besides myself, of McKnight, my brother, John G. James, David Kirker, William Shearer, Alexander Howard, Benjamin Potter, John Ivy, and François Malsaw, a Spaniard. Two men joined us after starting, Frederick Hector at the mouth of the Ohio and James Wilson in the Cherokee country, making eleven in all, young and daring men, eager for excitement and adventure. Ascending the Arkansas, the first settlement we reached was Eau Post, inhabited principally by French.[51]

A few days afterwards we arrived in the country of the Quapaws, where we met with a French-

[51]The American frontiersman mishandled the French language with cheerful abandon. "Eau Post" was not "Water Post," but was intended for the French term "au Post," meaning at, or to the Post. In English it might be spelled "O Post", as in Arent S. DePeyster's rhymed speech of July 4, 1779 to the Ottawa Indians at l'Arbe Croche, Michigan. Thus Peoria in Illinois became transformed by the same chronicler into "Pey," and by the furtraders generally into "Opa" or "Opee." James' "Eau Post" was Arkansas Post; originally established by Henry de Tonty in 1686, about forty miles above the mouth of the Arkansas, it is the oldest white settlement in the Mississippi Valley. In 1721 it was made the administrative center of the Arkansas District, one of nine subdivisions of the province of Louisiana. Following the admission of Louisiana to statehood in 1812, Arkansas District was joined with Missouri Territory. When the latter applied for statehood in 1819, it became a separate territory with Arkansas Post as the first Capital. During the Civil War a Union army 30,000 strong, aided by Admiral Porter's fleet of river ironclads, compelled the surrender of the Post on January 11, 1863.

man named Veaugean, an old man of considerable
wealth, who treated us with hospitality. His son
had just returned from hunting with a party of
Quapaws and had been attacked by the Pawnees,
who killed several of his Indian companions. Pawnee was then the name of all the tribes that are
now known as Comanches. I had never known or
heard of any Indians of that name before I visited
their country on my way to Santa Fe. The Americans previously knew them only as Pawnees.[52]

The account brought by Veaugean's son surprised me, as we had heard that all the Indians
on our route were friendly. Leaving Veaugean's,[53]
we proceeded up the river through a very fertile
country. Dense and heavy woods of valuable timber lined both sides of the river, both below Eau
Post and above as far as we went, and the river
bottoms, which are large, were covered by extensive cane-brakes, which appeared impenetrable

[52]Whatever the contemporary usage known to James
may have been, the Pawnees and the Comanches were entirely distinct tribes. Among the stated objectives of Zebulon M. Pike's 1806-1807 expedition were to establish
peace between the Pawnees of Kansas and the Osages, and
to open friendly relations with remoter Comanches and
other southwestern tribes. The Comanches were a branch
of the Shoshonean family and a comparatively recent offshoot from the Shoshone of Wyoming. The Pawnees belonged to the Caddoan family. Both were Plains Indians.
[53]Veaugean's home was about four miles below Pine
Bluff, Arkansas.

even by the rattlesnake. Small fields of corn, squash, and pumpkins, cultivated by Indians, appeared in view on the low banks of the river.

Since entering the Arkansas we had found the country quite level; after sailing and pushing about three hundred miles from the mouth we now reached the first high land near Little Rock, the capital of the Territory, as established that spring. The archives had not yet been removed from Eau Post, the former capital. As we approached Little Rock we beheld a scene of true western life and character that no other country could present. First we saw a large wood and stone building in flames, and then about one hundred men, painted, masked, and disguised in almost every conceivable manner, engaged in removing the town. These men, with ropes and chains, would march off a frame house on wheels and logs, place it about three or four hundred yards from its former site, and then return and move off another in the same manner. They all seemed tolerably drunk, and among them I recognized almost every European language spoken. They were a jolly set indeed. Thus they worked amid songs and shouts, until by night-fall they had completely changed the site of their town. Such buildings as they could not move they burned down, without a dissentant voice.

The occasion of this strange proceeding was as

follows: The Territorial Court was then in session at Diamond Hill, about thirty miles distant on the river above, and the news had reached Little Rock on the morning of our arrival that a suit pending in this Court and involving the title to the town, wherein one Russell of St. Louis was the claimant, had gone against the citizens of Little Rock and in favor of Russell.[54] The whole community instantly turned out en masse and in one day and night Mr. Russell's land was disencumbered of the town of Little Rock. They coolly and quietly, though not without much unnecessary noise, took the town up and set it down on a neighboring claim of the Quapaw tribe, and fire removed what was irremovable in a more convenient way. The free and enlightened citizens of Little Rock made a change of landlords more rapidly than Bonaparte took Moscow.

Here I saw Matthew Lyon, then quite an old man, canvassing for Congress.[55] He was a man of

[54]In 1820 some Missourians laid out a town which they named Arkopolis. William Russell, a Virginian who migrated to St. Louis, claimed title to the ground and in 1821 he and associates laid out the town of Little Rock, with consequences which James' party arrived in time to witness. Russell's home at Ninth and Russell Streets, St. Louis was still standing although in ruins, in 1916. A portion of his private library is now owned by the Missouri Historical Society. Douglas, 100–102.

[55]Matthew Lyon's career and character deserve a much longer recital than our present space permits. A native of

some note in John Adams' administration, by whom he was imprisoned under the Alien and Sedition law. He came into Little Rock with the judge and lawyers from Diamond Hill, the day

Ireland, he migrated to America in boyhood, paying the cost of his passage by a three-year term of service. Extraordinarily aggressive and energetic, and possessed of marked talent for business affairs, he is remembered chiefly for his stormy political career. He pioneered on two frontiers-Lake Champlain-Vermont and Kentucky-Arkansas—served actively in the Revolution, and long years in Congress. A thorough-going democrat, he commonly maintained a critical attitude toward the party in power, and from this much of his political and personal vicissitudes stemmed. Defeated for reelection to Congress and financially ruined, President Monroe in 1820 appointed him factor to the Cherokee Nation.

He established his headquarters at Spadra Bluff, which in the subsequent era of settlement of Arkansas became a popular point of debarkation for settlers who came up the Arkansas by steamboat. Spadra became a thriving town, the aspirant for the location of the county seat. In subsequent decades it was overshadowed by the present nearby city of Clarksville, and it is now (1953) a mere hamlet.

Lyon died and was buried at Spadra Bluff, August 1, 1822, where his abandoned grave site may still be seen. In 1830 his remains were removed to Eddyville, Kentucky, for reinterment. The local historian relates that in anticipation of such removal, Lyons had had a double coffin prepared for his burial, one box inside the other with the space between them filled with lime and the inner box lined with beaten lead. At the reburial in 1830, when the coffin was opened his face was seen for a brief moment as natural as in life, when it crumbled to dust before the eyes of the assembled family and friends. See Ella M. Langford, *Johnson County Arkansas: the First Hundred Years* (Clarksville, 1921) pp. 9–10.

after the grand moving of the town. He rode a
mule, which had thrown him into a bayou, and
his appearance as he came in, covered with mud
from head to foot, was a subject of much laughter
for his companions and the town of Little Rock,
which had now begun to assume a look of some
age, being just twenty-four hours old. Lyon was
not returned to Congress and he died a few years
afterwards. In 1824 I saw his grave at Spadra, in
the Cherokee country, where he had kept a trading establishment.

Before I left Little Rock I procured a license to
trade with all the Indian tribes on the Arkansas
and its tributaries, from Secretary Charles Crittenden, Governor Miller being out of the Territory.[56] I gave bond in the sum of $3000, with Judge

[56]The newly-appointed Governor was Colonel James
Miller of New Hampshire who had won distinction as a
soldier in the War of 1812. At Lundy's Lane, when asked
by General Ripley if he could silence a British battery he
replied "I'll try sir," and successfully stormed the position. Earlier in the war, as Colonel of the Fourth U. S.
Regiment, General Hull's sole regular force at Detroit,
Miller had won distinction as the victor of Mongaugon, the
only success in Hull's ill-fated campaign. His answer to
General Ripley at Lundy's Lane became an army slogan,
and the subject of subsequent textbook fame. Governor
Miller arrived in considerable state at Arkansas Post in a
barge which had been fitted up for the conveyance from
Pittsburgh at the close of December, 1819. Meanwhile
Robert Crittenden, the twenty-two year old Territorial
Secretary had assembled the Legislature on July 28 and

Scott[57] as security, to observe the laws of the United States, and it always appeared to me that I
was entitled to indemnity from my country for
the robberies which I suffered from the Indians.
My losses in this way were tremendous and have
weighed me down to the earth from that day to
this, the best portion of my life; but not one cent
have I ever been able to obtain from the justice of
Congress, whose laws I was bound to obey, whose
license from the hands of a government officer I
carried with me, and who by every rule of justice
was bound to protect me in a business which it
authorized by license and regulated by heavy
penalties.

Continuing our course up the river, we passed
through a more rocky and uneven country than

set the wheels of local government in motion. Governor
Miller was absent during much of his term of office, and
Crittenden, who continued as Secretary for ten years,
assumed the duties of acting-governor. He died in Vicks-
burg, Dec. 18, 1834, "exhausted by an argument of seven
hours' duration." Crittenden was a brother of John J.
Crittenden, noted Kentucky political leader.

[57]Judge Andrew Scott was a native of Virginia. He became a lawyer and about the year 1805 settled in Washington County, Missouri, which remained his home until his
appointment by President Monroe in 1818 as one of the
three judges of the Board of Governor and Judges of
Arkansas Territory. Unlike many such territorial appoin-
tees, Judge Scott was an able and sincere person, who
accepted and discharged the responsibilities of his position. He died March 13, 1851 in Pope County, Arkansas.

that below Little Rock. The Maumel Mountain, some fifty or sixty miles above this town and a mile from the south bank of the river, is a great curiosity.[58] It rises six hundred feet above the level of the river, and in shape resembles a coal-pit. A large spring of fresh water gushes from the top and runs down its side to the river. We now passed through the country of the Cherokees, whose farms and log houses made a fine appearance on the banks of the river, and would compare favorably with those of any western State. They were at this time highly civilized and have since made great advances in the arts. These were that part of the nation called the Rogers party, who had just emigrated from the east to the west side of the Mississippi, and ultimately, about the year 1833, with the powerful agency of the General Government, caused the removal of the whole nation to this country, where they are making rapid progress in national prosperity. Their Delegate will take his seat in our next Congress as Representative of the first Indian Territory ever organized. If this

[58]Thomas Nuttall, whose *Journal of Travels into the Arkansa Territory During the Year 1819* . . . was published at Philadelphia in 1821, made two striking drawings of the mamelle, which he described as presenting "the appearance of a vast pyramid, hiding the summit in the clouds." It is in Pulaski County, a few miles above Little Rock, at the junction of Maumelle Creek with the Arkansas. Note that here, as frequently elsewhere, James' estimates of distances are inaccurate.

nation shall form a nucleus for the preservation
of the race from annihilation, the cheerless pre-
dictions of the physiologists will be most fortunately falsified, and the philanthropist will rejoice
in the perpetuation of the true Indian race and
character.

Fort Smith lies about six hundred miles from
the mouth of the Arkansas on the western con-
fines of the Cherokee country, and near that of
the Osages, which tribes were now at war with
each other. We stopped a few days at this post,
where we were well received by Lieutenant Scott
and the commandant, Major Bradford, who examined and approved our license.[59] The Major

[59]Fort Smith was established in 1817 by Major Stephen
H. Long, who had been ordered to select a site for a military post near the border of the Indian country. He chose
the point of land lying between the Poteau and the Arkansas rivers, at the extreme western border of Arkansas.
It was named for General Thomas A. Smith, a Virginian,
who attained the rank of brigadier general in the War of
1812, and upon the reorganization of the army in 1815
was commissioned Colonel of the Rifle Regiment.

The first commandant of the fort was Major William
Bradford, whom James encountered. Its erection was carried out under his supervision. The fort was a picketed
stockade, with blockhouses at the corners. A report of
September, 1820 shows that but two sides of the stockade
had been completed. Major Bradford commanded the fort
until 1822. He died at Fort Towson, Oct. 20, 1826. In
April, 1824 the garrison of Fort Smith was removed to
Fort Coffee, a few miles farther up the Arkansas.

Martin Scott, renowned for his markmanship, entered

FORT SMITH IN 1853

Drawn by H. B. Mollhausen, Artist of Survey of a Railroad Route to the Pacific.

was a small, stern-looking man, an excellent disciplinarian, and a gallant officer. He invited McKnight and me to make his house our home until we had rested our company and put our guns in good order preparatory to entering the Indian country. He and his wife treated us with the utmost kindness and hospitality, and on leaving, presented us a large supply of garden vegetables, with a barrel of onions which we were not to broach until we had killed our first buffalo, when we were enjoined to have "a general feast in honor of old Billy Bradford." His kindness made a deep impression on us.

We here tried to mark out our course for the future, which we determined should be the Arkansas to within sixty miles from Taos in New Mexico, Baum having told me that this river was navigable thus far, and the Canadian being too shallow for our boat. Parting from the hospitable old Major, we ascended the river to the Salt Fork, which enters from the south, passing in our way the Grand River, then called the Six Bulls, and the Verdigris, at whose mouth Fort Gibson has

the army from Vermont in 1814 and served continuously on the northwestern and other frontiers until he was killed in the battle of Molino del Rey, Mexico, Sept. 8, 1847. The stories told of his markmanship are well-nigh incredible. Colonel Randolph B. Marcy's *Thirty Years of Army Life on the Border,* published in 1866, devotes a chapter to Scott's career.

since been built.[60] The waters of the Salt Fork are very much saturated with salt, tasting like strong brine where they enter the Arkansas. After this we proceeded with great difficulty, and about thirty miles above the Salt Fork our farther progress was entirely stopped by the lowness of the water.

There being no prospect of a speedy rise in the river at this time, which was the month of August, we returned four miles to an Osage road, which we had observed in going up, and here I sent three men to the Osage village, which I knew could not be far distant, for the purpose of opening a trade with this tribe. In five or six days these

[60]James' "Salt Fork" was the Cimarron River, which rises in the Raton Mountains near the Colorado-New Mexico border and flows generally southeasterly to its junction with the Arkansas in northeastern Oklahoma. His "Grand River" was the Neosho, which rises in Morris County in east-central Kansas, some distance south of Wichita and joins the Arkansas close to the mouths of the Cimarron and the Verdigris.

Fort Gibson was established by Colonel Matthew Arbuckle in April, 1824, about two miles above the mouth of the Neosho. Jefferson Davis was stationed here during the closing months of his regular army career in 1834-35. Douglas (p. 107) relates a local legend to the effect that the house Davis and his wife occupied at Fort Gibson was for many years an object of great interest, and was finally carried away, "even the foundation stones" by relic hunters. Their zeal was misapplied. Davis had no wife while stationed at Fort Gibson. He married Miss Taylor (his first wife) at Louisville following his resignation from the army, and she died three months later at his Mississippi home, never having seen, or been near, Fort Gibson.

men returned to me with forty Osages and a Capt.
Pryor, formerly of the United States army. I mentioned him in the first chapter as the commander
of the escort of the Mandan chief, Shehaka. He was
a Sergeant in Lewis and Clark's expedition, and a
captain at the battle of New Orleans. On the re-
duction of the army after the war he was discharged to make way for some parlor soldier and
sunshine patriot, and turned out in his old age
upon the "world's wide common." I found him
here among the Osages, with whom he had taken
refuge from his country's ingratitude and was
living as one of their tribe, where he may yet be
unless death has discharged the debt his country
owed him.

I took out some goods, and with McKnight,
my brother, and the Spaniard, Malsaw, accompanied Capt. Pryor and the Indians to their village, to the southeast, which we reached in two
days.[61] Here we found our old friend, Major
Bradford, Hugh Glenn, from Cincinnati, with

[61]This was in Mayes County, Oklahoma, on the west
side of the Verdigris River. It had been established by a
party of Osages early in the nineteenth century whom
Pierre Chouteau induced to leave their former home on
the Little Osage of Missouri when Manuel Lisa obtained
from the Spanish government the trade monopoly of the
Osages. In Oklahoma the band waged war upon the Cherokees and for many years proved a source of trouble to
the U. S. Government. Pryor Creek and the town of Pryor
preserve the memory of Captain Pryor's residence here.

goods and about twenty men on his way to the
Spanish country, and also Capt. Barbour, an Indian trader from the mouth of the Verdigris, and
formerly of Pittsburgh.[62] I proposed to Glenn,
whom I shall have to mention unfavorably here-
after, to travel in company to the Spanish country; but he appearing averse to the arrangement,
I did not urge it upon him.[63]

I bought twenty-three horses of the Osages at

[62]Concerning Captain Barbour, but little has been
learned aside from what James records. Grant Foreman
states (*Pioneer Days in the Southwest* (Cleveland, 1926),
52), that he had a trading establishment in partnership
with George W. Brand, at the mouth of the Verdigris.
This was sold to Colonel A. P. Chouteau, probably shortly
before Barbour's descent to New Orleans and death, as related by James, *post,* p. 214, which occurred in 1823.
Foreman, *Ibid,* 75.

[63]Hugh Glenn, who figures prominently and unfavorably in James' subsequent narration, was born of Scotch
ancestry in Berkeley County, Virginia (now West Virginia) January 7, 1788 and died in Cincinnati, May 28,
1833. He migrated to Kentucky in early manhood and
eventually established his permanent home in Cincinnati.
His active career was largely passed as a trader and army
contractor, in the course of which he made extensive
journeys throughout the western country. For some time
he maintained a trading post at the mouth of the Verdigris River, and from nearby Fort Smith in 1821 he made
the journey to Santa Fe which figures in James' narrative.
He returned to St. Louis in July, 1822. Jacob Fowler of
Kentucky, who was second in command, kept a journal of
the expedition which was published in 1898 under the
editorship of Elliott Coues, and which sheds considerable
incidental light upon James' own experiences.

high prices for packing my goods and agreed with Barbour to *cache* (hide in the earth) my heaviest and least portable goods near the Arkansas, for him to take in the following spring down to his store at the mouth of the Verdigris, sell them, and account to me for the proceeds on my return. I returned with my companions to the river and carefully concealed my flour, whiskey, lead, hardware, and other heavy goods. I showed Capt. Pryor, who came up the next day with a party of Osages going out on their fall hunt, the place where I had hid these goods, and packing the rest on my horses, we left the Arkansas to our right, or the north, and travelled with Pryor and the Indians for two days toward the southwest. We then left them[64] and bore directly to the west in the direction as pointed out to us by the Indians, of the Salt Plains and Shining Mountains.

In eleven days we struck the Salt Fork, mentioned before, and which is set down on the latest maps as the Cimarron River. In the distance before us we discerned the bright mountains before mentioned, which the Indians had

[64]Pryor accompanied Glenn upon the latter's expedition to Santa Fe. Jacob Fowler's *Journal* of the Glenn expedition states that on June 22, 1822 Pryor and two others left Glenn's party to join that of James. Coues, Fowler's editor, fixes this departure, which occurred on the return from Santa Fe, as taking place near Ford, Kansas, a few miles east of Dodge City.

directed us to pass in our route. We held on our course for two days along the right bank of the Salt Fork, over mounds and between hills of sand which the wind had blown up in some places to the height of one hundred feet.[65] Our progress was very slow, the horses sometimes sinking to their breasts in the sand. The bed of the river in many places was quite dry, the water being lost in the sand, and as we advanced it appeared covered over with salt, like snow. The water, mantled over with salt, stood in frequent pools, from the bottom of which we could scoop up that mineral in bushels. The channel of the Salt River became narrower and more shallow as we proceeded. The sand so obstructed our progress that we crossed

[65]From the Osage town in Mayes County, James' party evidently traveled westward across Rogers (vicinity of Claremore), Tulsa, and Osage counties to the Arkansas somewhere above the mouth of the Cimarron. From here it traveled generally westward to the "Shining Mountains" in northern Major County, the narrative making it impossible to trace its course with any degree of precision. Somewhere above the "Shining Mountains" James crossed to the North Fork of the Canadian, which above its junction with Wolf Creek in northwestern Woodward County is commonly called Beaver Creek, although James continues to call it the Canadian. General Custer's Camp Supply, which figures prominently in *My Life on the Plains,* the Lakeside Classics volume for 1952, was at the junction of Wolf and Beaver creeks, and the town of Supply, nearby, still preserves its name. In ascending the Beaver (as we suppose) James passed into the extreme northwestern extension of Oklahoma, formerly known as the Cherokee Strip.

the river where traveling was less difficult, and soon struck a branch of the Salt Fork, equally impregnated with salt as the main stream. Large crusts of salt lay at the water's edge. Proceeding on we came to the Shining Mountains, and a high hill evidently based upon salt. It stands near the salt branch, the banks of which were composed of salt rocks, from which the men broke off large pieces with their tomahawks. Here, and in the Salt River was enough of this valuable mineral to supply the world for an indefinite period.

The Shining Mountains lay south of us about four miles and had been visible for several days. We visited them and found one of the greatest curiosities in our country. I have never seen them nor the salt plains in which they stand put down on any map or described by any white man.[66] All of our travellers in this region appear to have passed to the north or south of them, as I have never seen or heard of a description of them, except by the Indians, who come here regularly and in great force for salt. The mountains stand separate from each other, are about three hun-

[66]Unknown to James, John Bradbury's Journal of *Travels in the Interior of America in the years 1809, 1810, and 1811* . . . published in London in 1819, contained a description of the Grand Saline and the Shining Mountains, as recorded by George C. Sibley, the U. S. Factor at Fort Osage, who visited the area in the summer of 1811. For it see Thwaites (Ed.), *Early Western Travels,* V, 191–94.

dred feet in height, and are quite flat on the summit. They are composed, in part, of a shining, semi-transparent rock which reflects the rays of the sun to a great distance. It is soft, being easily cut with a knife, and the hand is visible through thin pieces of it when held in the sun light. They extend about thirty miles on the left of Salt River in a northwest and southeast direction, are all of an equal height, containing an area on the top of from ten rods to a hundred acres, and are entirely destitute of timber. The tops of most of them were inaccessible. With great difficulty we ascended one of about ten acres in extent, from which we saw along the tops of the others, they all being on the same plane. We found the short thin grass of the prairie below, but no shrub except the prickly pear. The ground was covered with immense quantities of buffalo manure, when left there it would be vain to conjecture. The substance from the ground was clay for upwards of two hundred feet, then came the rock from ten to twenty feet thick, projecting over the earth, and the soil above was about ten feet in depth. The rock is fast crumbling away by the action of water, which seems to dissolve it, as we found very few fragments at the foot of the mountains and none of any considerable size. The whole country was evidently at one time on a level with these singular elevations.

We continued our course up the bank of the same branch of Salt River by which we had come. Its water was now, after leaving the salt plains, fresh and wholesome, and we travelled along its bank two days, when finding it took us too much to the north, we left it and bore to the southwest. This was the sixth day after reaching the Salt Fork, and seventeen after parting with Capt. Pryor and the Osages. We killed seven buffaloes after leaving the Shining Mountains, and dried the meat. The carcasses of the buffaloes, attracting the buzzards, with some old shoes and other small articles left on the ground by the men, served to discover us to a war party of Comanches who were now on our trail. After leaving the Salt Branch we travelled till near night without finding wood or water and then bore again to the northwest till we struck the Branch. We cooked our meat with fuel of buffalo manure, which we gathered for the purpose.

Towards morning we were all alarmed by the barking of our dogs, followed by a clapping noise and the sound of footsteps. We slept no more on that night, and in the morning saw upwards of a hundred Indians at a short distance coming with the design of intercepting our horses, which were some distance from the camp. One horse was pierced by a lance. I exhibited the flag, which diverted their course, and they came among us in a very hostile manner, seizing whatever they could lay their hands on. The interpreter told us they were a war party and advised me to make peace with them by giving them presents. I did so, distributing about three thousand dollars worth of goods among them.

There were two chiefs in this party, one of whom was friendly and the other, called the One-eyed Chief, seemed determined to take our lives. His party, however, was in a minority and soon after went off. The friendly chief then came up to me and on account of his interference in our behalf demanded more presents, which I made to him. He told me that if I came to the village I should be well treated and implored me not to go up the Arkansas. I afterwards learned that the One-eyed Chief had left me with the purpose of waylaying us on that river and taking our lives, which was the reason of the friendly chief's advice. Those who were hostile, and they were the whole of the One-eyed Chief's party, seemed perfectly infuriated against us. They scrutinized our equipments, and said we had Osage horses and were spies of that nation, with whom they were then at war. At last we were rid of the presence of these unpleasant visitors with many dismal apprehensions for the future.

The friendly chief left a Mexican Indian, an interpreter, with us as a guide. With him we

struck from the south branch of Salt River for the
north Fork of the Canadian, which the Indians
told us we should reach in one day's travel. Going in a direction west of south we struck the
river on the second day, having suffered dreadfully for want of water. McKnight and I went forward to find water and killed a buffalo. We drank
large draughts of the blood of this animal, which I
recollect tasted like milk. We found several ponds
of water, so tainted with buffalo manure as to
cause us to vomit on drinking of it. We missed
the party on that night and found them on the
next day, all sick from the water they had drunk,
and exhausted by previous fatigue and thirst. The
horses were nearly worn out by the same causes.

We traveled along the North Fork of the Canadian for seven or eight days until we reached its
head in a large morass, or swamp, about two miles
wide and five or six long, situated in a valley
which gradually narrows and disappears at last
in the vast plain to the west.[67] We went up this
valley which was now dry, but in the spring is
filled with a rapid stream. We saw thousands of
buffaloes along its course and found a large pond
about an acre in extent, but the water was so

[67] The North Canadian or Beaver rises much farther to
the west than the party had yet reached. James' own
further statement of the dry valley which in wet seasons
became a rapid stream is indicative of this.

spoiled by manure as to sicken us all. After passing through this valley we bore for the Canadian River towards the south and on the second day, after intense suffering from thirst, we struck a fine spring of fresh water. This was a rich source of real refreshment and enjoyment.

Following the stream made by this spring, we reached the Canadian and travelled up its course for several days. We had encamped for the night on the twenty-first day after meeting the Comanches who had robbed us on the branch of Salt River, when we saw a great number of mounted Indians coming over a rising ground in our front, and at their head the friendly chief, who advanced with outstretched hands crying *towaue, towaue,*—"good, good." Coming up, he embraced me in the Indian custom, and requested me to go with him to his village.[68] Here an Indian seized a brass kettle and rode off with it. This act alarmed me, and I asked the chief if he could protect my property if I went with him. He said he could not, and I declined his invitation for that night and requested him to leave a body of trusty Indians, to defend me till morning. He did so, and we were not molested that night.

[68] This encounter with the Comanches occurred somewhere in the Texas Panhandle. In the same general area General Custer half a century later met and conquered the descendants of the natives who robbed and terrorized James' party.

In the morning we marched with our guard from the left bank of the river, where we had encamped, to the right bank, and in two miles above we found the whole village of the Indians, numbering a thousand lodges, situated in the bottom near the base of a large mound. We were met by one of the principal chiefs, whose looks were to me ominous of evil. He was a little, vicious-looking old man and eyed me most maliciously. We were taken close to the foot of the mound near this chief's lodge and there we encamped, having piled up my goods and covered them with skins. The Indians then demanded presents and about a thousand chiefs and warriors surrounded us. I laid out for them tobacco, powder, lead, vermillion, calico, and other articles, amounting to about $1,000 in value. This did not satisfy them and they began to break open my bales of cloth and divide my finest woolens, designed for the Spanish market, among them. After losing about $1000 more in this way, I induced them to desist from further robbery.

The principal chief, named Big Star, now appeared and said they had enough. They divided the spoil among two or three thousand, of whom all got some. They tore up the cloth into garments for the middle and blankets. They tied the silk handkerchiefs to their hair as ornaments, which streamed in the wind. This robbery over, I smoked with them and prepared to go on my journey. This they forbade, and we were compelled to stay over that day. We kept a strong guard through the night on our goods and horses. On the next morning they pretended that another party had arrived who required presents. This information was brought by a one-eyed Spaniard who acted as interpreter and had got from me as a present a whole suit of cloth and a large supply of ammunition. He was the instigator of this new demand. The Indians began to gather around us and break open and drag about the goods. The chiefs stood off, taking no part. I then made them another set of presents, worth, probably, a thousand dollars more. We now hoped to be allowed to pass on and requested leave to go, but they refused it and the friendly chief advised us to stay. I had seen many savages, but none so suspicious and little as these. They seemed to regard us as spies in their country. We staid with them the second day and night without any further robbery than that I have mentioned.

On the third day of my stay, the One-eyed Chief came into the village from the Arkansas, where he had been, with a hundred men, awaiting us with murderous designs. On his coming in, the interpreter, Malsaw, ran to me, saying we should certainly be killed, and the women and

children ran from their lodges like chickens before a hawk. I had made the Big Star chief my
friend by presenting him with a splendid sword.
He now came up and took me into the little old
chief's lodge, saying I would be shot if I remained
out. Our time seemed nearly come. In the distance we saw the One-eyed with his troop approaching, all painted black and armed with
guns, bows and arrows, and lances. We were
eleven against a hundred at least, perhaps thousands. The Big Star sent a messenger to my
enemy and asked him what would satisfy him in
lieu of our lives. He replied that he must have for
each of his men as much cloth as his outstretched
arms would once measure; an equal quantity of
calico; powder, lead, vermillion, knives, beads,
looking glasses, &c., and for himself the sword
which he had seen on the south branch of Salt
River. I sent him word that I had not the vermillion, knives, beads, and looking glasses, nor the
sword, which I had presented to the Big Star. He
said the story about the sword was a lie, that I
had given it to Big Star to prevent him from getting it, and that he would have it or my scalp,
and as to the other articles he would take cloth
instead of them. The Big Star here sent to his
lodge for the sword, and taking it in his hand, he
pressed its side to his heart and then handed it to
me, saying: "Take it and send it to the One-eyed

Chief. You have no other way of saving your life and the lives of your people." I did as he advised, and measured off about five hundred yards of cloth and calicoe, of which the former cost me seven dollars per yard in Baltimore, and sent them to my deadly enemy.

This appeared to pacify him and again I proposed to go on my way. To this they again objected, saying that the whole village would go down the river in the morning, and we should then be permitted to part from them and continue our course up the river as before meeting with them. We had the horses brought up and prepared that evening for an early start in the morning. One-half kept guard while the rest of our party endeavored to sleep. But there was no rest for any of us on that most dismal night. This was the third sleepless night which we had passed with these ferocious savages, and we were nearly worn down by fatigue, anxiety, and watching. Before day-light a party of boys ascended the mound in our rear, and from the top stoned our company until they were dislodged and driven down by the exertions of the friendly chief. Uncertain of our fate and nearly exhausted, we awaited in sullen patience the issue of events. The sun as he rose seemed to wear an aspect of gloom and every thing portended evil to our little band. Six of my horses had been taken in the night, and

I ordered my men out to find and bring them back.

The friendly chief now came to me with great concern and dejection in his countenance and begged of me not to leave my station or allow the men to go out. "Keep together," said he, "or you will be killed. The men that go out will be murdered. Don't try to get back your horses." I saw that the whole army were preparing to decamp, and pulling down their lodges. Sometime after sunrise I perceived about fifty of the chiefs and older Indians going up onto the mound above us, in our rear, followed by a multitude of young warriors and boys. An old man turned and drove them back: the two friendly chiefs did not go up. Arrived at the top, this company formed the circle, sat down, and smoked. Then one of their number commenced what seemed to us, from his gestures, to be a violent harangue designed to inflame their passions. I told my company that this council would decide our fate. They asked me how I knew this. "If they come down," said I, "friendly, we shall have nothing to fear; but if sulky and out of humor, we have nothing to hope. Put your guns in good order and be prepared for the worst. We must sell our lives as dearly as possible." In this sentiment they all agreed with me, and we prepared to meet our fate, whatever it should be, like men. During this time the lodges, with the women and children, were fast disappearing and the men assembling before us on horseback and afoot, armed with guns, bows, and lances. The council on the hill, after an hour's consultation, descended, and we soon learned that our deaths were determined upon.

Those Indians who before were sociable were now distant and sulky. When spoken to by any of us they made no answer. The friendly chief and Big Star, who had taken no part in the council, now came and shook hands and bade us farewell. I besought them to stay with us; shaking their heads sorrowfully, they went away. The press in front now greatly increased. Nearly two thousand warriors stood before and around us with the evident intention of making an attack, and appeared to be awaiting the signal for the onslaught. We stood in a circle with our backs to the goods and saddles heaped up above all our heads and with our rifles raised to our breasts and our fingers on the triggers. We were also armed with knives and tomahawks. Old Jemmy Wilson seized an axe, having no gun, and swore he would hew his way as far as he could. Thus we stood, eleven against two thousand, with death staring us in the face. All seemed unwilling to commence the bloody work. The suspense was awful. I stood between John McKnight and my brother, and noticed their countenances. Mc-

Knight's face was white and his chin and lips were quivering. My brother, as brave a man as ever lived, looked desperate and determined. Not a man but seemed bent to die in arms and fighting, and none were overcome by fear.

Thus we stood near half an hour in deathly silence; at length the White Bear warrior, a chief dressed in a whole bear skin with the claws hanging over his hands, rode swiftly towards us through the crowd with his lance in his hand, as if to annihilate us at once; but seeing the dangerous position he was in, he stopped short about five paces from us and glared upon me with the most deadly malignity. Finding he could not reach me with his lance, he took out his pistol, examined the priming, tossed out the powder from the pan, re-primed, and again fixed his devlish eyes full upon me. But he saw that I could fire first, and he kept his pistol down.

Here McKnight first broke the dreadful silence, saying, "Let us commence. James, You will be the first one killed—this suspense is worse than death; the black chief is my mark." I said: "No, McKnight, let us forbear as long as they do; for us to begin is folly in the extreme; but as soon as a gun is fired, we must fire, rush in, and sell our lives as dearly as possible." Here Kirker walked out with his gun over his head, gave it up, and passed into the crowd unmolested. In a minute afterwards we heard a cry from a distance, approaching nearer and nearer, of *Tabbaho, Tabbaho.** This I supposed was on account of Kirker's surrender. The cry increased and spread throughout the crowd. Looking towards the southwest, whence the cry arose, while the White Bear's attention was withdrawn, I saw six horsemen riding at full speed, and as they came nearer we heard the words in Spanish, "save them! save them!" In a moment a Spanish officer rushed into our arms, exclaiming: "Thank God we are in time; you are all safe and unhurt." He said that he had heard of our danger by accident that morning, and ridden twenty miles to save us.

All the circumstances of our rescue we learned the next day. With joyous and thankful hearts for our escape from a death that five minutes before seemed inevitable, we prepared to depart with our preservers. I had bidden farewell, as I thought forever, to my wife, child, home, and all its endearments, and the thoughts of them were now overpowering to me. The Spaniards asked the Indians why they were going to kill us. They answered, that the Spanish governor at Santa Fe had commanded them not to let any Americans pass, but that we were determined to go in spite of them, so that to stop us and keep their promise to the Spanish Governor they thought they

*White men.

were compelled to take our lives. The Spaniards told them that this was under the government of Spain, but that they were now independent and free and brothers to the Americans. This was the first news I had heard of the Mexican revolution.

The two friendly chiefs now returned, and I showed the Spaniards our passport. The Indians brought in and delivered up four of my horses. The whole village, soon after the arrival of the Spaniards, went down the river; and our party, except Malsaw and myself, with two of the Spanish officers, started forward towards the Spanish camp, about twenty miles distant. We four remained behind to recover the two missing horses and then followed our companions. We were lost, at dark, among the cliffs bordering the river, where we made fire for cooking our suppers and encamped for the night.

Early the next morning we reached the Spanish encampment, where our party was awaiting us. As we approached the camp there came out to meet us a tall Indian of about seventy years of age, dressed in the complete regimentals of an American colonel, with blue coat, red sash, white pantaloons, epaulets, and sword. He advanced with an erect, military air and saluted us with great dignity and address. His eyes were still bright and piercing, undimmed in the least by age, and he had a high, noble forehead and

Roman nose. His whole port and air struck me forcibly as those of a real commander and a hero. After saluting us he handed me a paper which I read as follows, as nearly as I now remember:

"*This is to certify that Cordaro, a Chief of the* "*Comanches, has visited the fort at Natchitoches* "*with fifteen of his tribe; that he remained here two* "*weeks, and during the whole time behaved very* "*well. It is my request that all Americans who meet* "*him or any of his tribe should treat him and them* "*with great respect and kindness, as they are true* "*friends of the United States.*

JOHN JAMESON.
"*U. S. Indian Agent at Natchitoches on Red River.*"

This chief, Cordaro, was the cause of our being then in existence. He told us he had promised his "great friend at Natchitoches" that he would protect all Americans that came through his country, and he very earnestly requested us to inform his "great friend" that he had been as good as his word. On entering the encampment we found about fifty Spaniards and three hundred Comanche warriors, who had just returned from an expedition against the Navahoes, a tribe inhabiting the country west of Santa Fe and the mountains, and who were then at war with the Spaniards. On their return from this campaign this party had come from Santa Fe with their

Comanche allies into their country to hunt for buffaloes and had encamped the night before our rescue from the Comanches on the spot where we now found them. On the next morning a party of Indians belonging to this band were hunting their horses in the prairie and met another party from the army below, who had us in custody, engaged in the same manner, who informed them that their countrymen had taken a company of Americans prisoners and were going to kill them all that morning and divide their goods among the army; that the whole village was breaking up and preparing to go down the Canadian, and that the pulling down of the last lodge was to be the signal for our massacre.

On hearing this, the first party hastened back to their camp with the news, which brought out most of the young warriors to come down for a share of the plunder of my goods. The chief, Cordaro, went instantly, on hearing this account, to the Spanish officers, told them that a company of Americans were to be murdered that morning by his countrymen, mentioned the signal for the attack, said he was too old to ride fast or he would go himself to the rescue, and adjured them to mount and ride without sparing the horses, as not a moment was to be lost. Six of them mounted and rode as Cordaro had told them to do, and we saw their foaming steeds and heard the cry of

*Tabbaho—white men—*just in time to save us from extermination. A minute after would probably have been too late. Our determined attitude averted the blow and prolonged our time to the last moment, when our deliverers appeared; but without them, the next instant would have seen a volley of shot and arrows lay most of us low and the lance and tomahawk would have soon completed the work on us all.

Cordaro, the noble and true-hearted savage, appeared to rejoice at our escape as much as we. He desired particularly that his "great friend" at Natchitoches should hear of his agency in saving us, and I had to promise him repeatedly that I would surely inform Colonel Jameson, when I saw him, of the manner in which his friend, Cordaro, had performed his promise to him. If John Jameson be still alive and this page meet his eye, I shall have cause to felicitate myself in having at last kept my word to my Comanche preserver.[69]

[69] Hollywood at its best can scarcely improve upon this real life story. Somewhat extensive search among the more probable sources of information has failed to disclose any mention of Cordaro, and but one notice has been found of John Jameson. On Sept. 5, 1818 the Secretary of War addressed a circular letter to several governors and Indian agents, among the latter being Jameson. Printed in Carter (Ed.), *Territorial Papers of the United States,* XV, 431. The absence of Cordaro from the available records suggests the possibility that he may have had another name than the one James employs.

We spent that day with Cordaro and the Spaniards, and held a council or "talk" with them. Cordaro made a speech dissuading me from going to Santa Fe on account of the treatment which the Americans had always received from the Government there. "They will imprison you," said he to me, "as they have imprisoned all Americans that ever went to Santa Fe. You will meet the fate of all your countrymen before you." The Spanish officers, who were all present at this harangue, smiled and said there was no danger of any ill-treatment to us, now that they had an independent government. Cordaro shook his head incredulously and told them that we were under his protection; that he would himself go to Santa Fe after we had arrived there, and if he found us imprisoned he would immediately go to war with them. "The Americans are my friends," said he, "and I will not permit them to be hurt. I have promised my great friend of Natchitoches to protect all Americans that come through my country." The Spaniards promised to treat us well, but our protector seemed to be very suspicious of them and evidently gave little faith to their promises.

We found at this camp an excellent Spanish interpreter, who spoke the Comanche language as well as his own. By him I was informed that the Indians took me for the Frenchman Vaugean,

whom we had seen in the country of the Quapaws, a tribe of kin to the Osages, and who, while
hunting on the Canadian in the spring before
with a party of thirty French and Indians of the
former tribe, had been attacked by the Comanches, who were defeated and driven back with
considerable loss. Vaugean, like myself, was a tall
man, and the Indians here and those we had met
before considered me the commander in this battle. The one-eyed interpreter had concealed this
fact from me, and we now had some difficulty in
satisfying the Indians that we were not the same
party who, with Vaugean, were in alliance with
their enemies, the Osages. The charge was frequently renewed, but we at last succeeded in re-
pelling it and quieting their suspicions.

On the next day, the third day after meeting
with the Spanish officers, we parted with Cordaro,
who followed his countrymen down the Canadian, with the Spanish force in his company.
Two of the Spanish officers remained to accompany us to Santa Fe. They were all very gentlemanly and liberal-minded men. One Spanish
citizen of Santa Fe had hired to return with me as
a guide. We once more took up our march along
the Canadian and over the immense plains by the
trail of the Spaniards we had just parted with.
The whole country here is one immense prairie.
I observed many huge granite rocks standing like

stone buildings, some of them one hundred feet high. The earth seemed to have been washed from around them and the prairie below to have been formed by deposits of earth and crumbled rocks from these and similar elevations. Some were covered with earth and cedar trees, but most of them were entirely bare.

In three days after leaving Cordaro we came in sight of the Rocky Mountains, whose three principal peaks, covered with perpetual snow, were glittering in the sun. The most northern and highest of these peaks is set down on the latest map I have seen as "James' Peak or Pike's." General Pike endeavored to reach its top, but without success. After my return I made a rough map with a pen of this country for the use of Senator Kane of Illinois, and in the next map published by Government I saw my name affixed to this peak, as I supposed, by the agency of Mr. Kane. The peak bore no name known to our company when we saw it and I gave it none then or afterwards.[70]

[70] Here James' memory is doubly confused. He had been following the Canadian River across the Texas Panhandle into eastern New Mexico, and Pike's Peak was 200 miles or more to the northward. The mountains seen were evidently much farther south, somewhere in New Mexico, east of Sante Fe.

Pike's Peak was first ascended by an American, Dr. Edwin James, the narrator of Major Stephen H. Long's expedition to the Rocky Mountains, in July, 1820. Long

In two days more we came to an old Spanish
fort, dismantled and deserted, which had been
built many years before in expectation of an invasion from the United States. This was about
one hundred miles from Santa Fe. We soon encountered large herds of sheep, attended by
shepherds, and on the second day after passing
the fort came to a small town in a narrow ravine
on the Pecos River and at the foot of a high
cliff.[71] Here I became acquainted with an old

named the mountain (which Pike had made no effort to
ascend) in James' honor, and for some years it was known
indifferently as James' Peak and Pike's Peak. The coin-
cidence of identity of names is evidently responsible for
General James' confusion.

[71]The Pecos River, some 800 miles long, rises in the
Rocky Mountains, in San Miguel County, New Mexico,
and runs southward and eastward, roughly paralleling the
course of the Rio Grande, to its junction with the latter
near the 101° of longitude. James' party had now passed
from the headwaters of the Canadian to those of the Pecos.
The town alluded to was La Cuesta. It lay in a deep valley,
enclosed by high rocks, through the bottom of which the
headwaters of the Pecos wound, with the village lying
"like a little fortress" on a lower step of the plateau.
Baldwin Möllhausen, who in 1853 accompanied the expedition led by A. W. Whipple in search of a route for the
projected railroad to the Pacific, provides an interesting
picture of the town and its surroundings. See *Diary of a
Journey from the Mississippi to the Coasts of the Pacific*
(London, 1858), I, 316–20 and map. It was in La Cuesta
that Goerge W. Kendall and his party were captured in
1841 and saved from immediate execution through the
intercession of an influential citizen, Don Gregorio Vigil.

Spaniard, named Ortise, who in his youth had been captured by the Pawnees and sold to Chouteau of St. Louis, where he had learned French and whence he returned home by the way of New Orleans, St. Antonio in Texas, and the interior of Mexico. He informed me more particularly than I had yet heard of the Mexican Revolution, and foretold that Iturbide would be elected President at the ensuing election.[72]

We proceeded up the bank of the Pecos by a narrow road, impassable for wagons. One of the horses with all my powder and some of the most valuable goods here fell down a precipice into a beaver dam in the river. The horse was uninjured but the goods were nearly all spoiled. The next town on our route was San Miguel, fifteen miles from the last, an old Spanish town of about

Narrative of the Texan Sante Fe Expedition, the Lakeside Classics volume for 1929, pp. 375–85.

[72] Space is lacking to sketch the confused story of the Mexican revolution. The independence achieved in 1821 was the culmination of a decade of confusion and turmoil, and the introduction of a sixty-three-year period of further turmoil and warfare. Somewhat like our own movement to create the present U.S. Constitution, the Mexican movement for independence culminated in a counter-reaction against the more radical revolutionists, brought to successful conclusion by Iturbide, who was elected Emperor by the first provincial Congress, July 21, 1822. Further dissension led to his abdication and deportation in April, 1823, followed by his return to Mexico and his prompt execution, July 1, 1824.

a hundred houses, a large church, and two miserably-constructed flour mills. Here was the best water-power for mills, and the country in the vicinity abounded in the finest pine timber, I had ever seen. But no attempt is made to improve the immense advantages which nature offers. Every thing that the inhabitants were connected with seemed going to decay.[73]

We left San Miguel on the following morning with the alcalde and a company of Spaniards bound for Santa Fe. We stopped at night at the ancient Indian village of Pecos about fifteen miles from San Miguel. I slept in the fort, which encloses two or three acres in an oblong, the sides of which are bounded by brick houses three stories high, and without any entrances in front. The window frames were five feet long and three-fourths of a foot in width, being made thus narrow to prevent all ingress through them. The

[73] San Miguel was a considerable town and an important point on the route of the Santa Fe traders. Here George W. Kendall and his party were imprisoned, following their capture in the summer of 1841, and here they witnessed the summary execution by command of Governor Armijo of Samuel Howland, another member of the expedition. See *The Texan Santa Fe Expedition*, the Lakeside Classics volume for 1929, pp. 404–11. A view of the town and its surroundings in 1846 is given in Wm. H. Emory's *Notes of a Military Reconnoissance from Fort Leavenworth in Missouri to San Diego in California*, 30th Cong., 1 sess., Exec. Doc. 41, p. 444.

lights were made of isinglass and each story was supplied with similar windows. A balcony surmounted the first and second stories and movable ladders were used in ascending to them on the front. We entered the fort by a gate which led into a large square. On the roofs, which like those of all the houses in Mexico are flat, were large heaps of stones for annoying an enemy. I noticed that the timbers, which extended out from the walls about six feet and supported the balconies, were all hewn with stone hatchets. The floors were of brick, laid on poles, bark, and mortar. The brick was burned in the sun and made much larger than ours, being about two feet by one. The walls were covered with plaster made of lime and isinglass.

I was informed by the Spaniards and Indians that this town and fort are of unknown antiquity, and stood there in considerable splendor in the time of the Conquerors. The climate being dry and equable and the wood in the buildings the best of pine and cedar, the towns here suffer but little by natural decay. The Indians have lost all tradition of the settlement of the town of Pecos.[74]

[74]The pueblo of Pecos has an ancient and slowly declining history. In prehistoric times a series of puebloes were scattered along the Pecos Valley from Anton Chico to the northern end of the Pecos grant. At the time of Coronado's visit (1541) the tribe was concentrated in a great communal structure having 2000 to 2500 inhabit-

It stood a remarkable proof of the advance made by them in the arts of civilization before the Spaniards came among them. All the houses are well built and showed marks of comfort and refinement. The inhabitants, who were all Indians, treated us with great kindness and hospitality. In the evening I employed an Indian to take my horses to pasture, and in the morning when he brought them up I asked him what I should pay him. He asked for powder and I was about to give him some when the Spanish officer forbade me, saying it was against the law to supply the Indians with ammunition. Arms are kept out of their hands by their masters, who prohibit all trade in those articles with any of the tribes around them.

On the next day in the evening we came in sight of Santa Fe, which presented a fine appearance in the distance. It is beautifully situated on a plain of dry and rolling ground, at the foot of a high mountain, and a small stream which rises in the mountain to the west runs directly through the city. It contained a population at this time of

ants and popularly called Pecos. The great church, a landmark on the Santa Fe Trail, was erected about the year 1617. Epidemics and Apache and Comanche warfare reduced the population until in 1838 the 17 survivors abandoned the pueblo and removed to Jemez. Data adapted from Hodge, *Handbook of American Indians North of Mexico.*

VIEW OF SANTA FE IN 1846

Reproduced from drawing in Lieut. Col. Wm. H. Emory's Notes of a Military Reconnoissance from Fort Leavenworth in Missouri to San Diego in California . . . Made in 1846-7 with the Advanced Guard of the "Army of the West."

six thousand. The houses were all white-washed outside and in, and presented a very neat and pleasing sight to the eye of the traveller. They are all flat on the roof and most of them one story in height. There are five very splendid churches, all Roman Catholic, which are embellished with pictures, and ornaments of gold and silver in the most costly style. The chalices were of pure gold and candlesticks of silver.

The principal buildings, including the fort, are built around the public square in the middle of the city. The fort, which occupies the whole side of this square, encloses about ten acres, and is built on the plan of the Pecos fort above described. There is an outer wall about eight feet in height enclosing the buildings, which like those at Pecos bound the inner square. The whole was falling to decay and but few soldiers were stationed in it. The farms are without fences or walls, and the cattle, hogs, &c. have to be confined during the raising and harvesting of crops. They raise onions, peas, beans, corn, wheat, and red pepper—the last a principal ingredient in Spanish food. Potatoes and turnips were unknown. I saw peach trees, but none of apples, cherries, or pears. The gardens were enclosed.

The country is entirely destitute of rain except in the months of June and July, when the rivers are raised to a great height. A continual drought prevails throughout all the rest of the year, not even relieved by dews. Consequently the ground has to be irrigated by means of the many streams which rise in the mountains and flow into the Rio Grande, and for this purpose canals are cut through every farm. Land that can be watered is of immense value, while that which is not near the streams is worthless. While in Santa Fe, a Spaniard took me sixteen miles south, to show me his farm of 15 acres, for which he had just paid $100 per acre, and which lay conveniently to water. Hogs and poultry are scarce, while sheep, goats, and cattle are very abundant.

CHAPTER IV
Sojourn at Santa Fe

I ENTERED Santa Fe on the first day of December, 1821, and immediately went with Ortise as interpreter to the Governor's *palatia* or house, to whom I made known my object in visiting his country and showed my passport. He remarked on reading it that they were entirely independent of Spain, that the new government had not laid any duties on imports, and gave me permission to vend my goods. I rented a house, and on the next day commenced business. In about two weeks I took in $200, which I advanced to John McKnight for the expenses of his journey to Durango, about sixteen hundred miles south, where his brother Robert was living after his enlargement from prison. They both returned in the month of April following. Soon after McKnight's departure, I heard of Hugh Glenn's arrival at Taos, sixty miles north of Santa Fe and was soon after favored with a visit from him. He came down to Santa Fe, borrowed $60 from me, and at the end of a week returned to Taos.

About six weeks after I reached Santa Fe my true friend and protector, Cordaro, came in according to promise, with thirty of his tribe, to ascertain if we were at liberty. He was dressed in his full regimentals and commanded the respect of the Spanish officials, who behaved towards him with great deference. By his request a council was held, which convened in the Spanish Council House on the public square and was attended by the Spanish officers, magistrates, and principal citizens of Santa Fe. Cordaro made the speech for which he had caused the council to be held. He expressed his pleasure at finding that we and the Spaniards were friends, that he would be pleased to see us always living together like brothers, and hoped that the American trade would come to his country as well as to the Spaniards. He complained that we traded with their enemies, the Osages, and furnished them with powder, lead, and guns, but had no intercourse with the Comanches. He hoped the government of the United States would interfere and stop the depredations of the Osages upon his nation. "They steal our horses and murder our people," said he, "and the Americans sell them the arms and ammunition which they use in war upon us. We want your trade, and if you will come among us we will not cheat nor rob you. I have had a talk with my nation and told them they had done a great wrong in treating you as they did, and they promised never to do so again. They say they will pay you in horses and mules for the goods they

took from you on the Canadian, if you will only
come once more into our country. Come with
your goods among us; you shall be well treated. I
pledge you my word, the word of Cordaro, that
you shall not be hurt nor your goods taken from
you without full payment. Each of my nation
promises to give you a horse if you will come and
trade with us once more, and though poor, and
though I got none of your goods, yet will I give
you two of the best horses in the nation. Come to
our country once more and you shall find friends
among the Comanches. Come and you shall be
safe. Cordaro says it."

The old warrior spoke like an orator and
looked like a statesman. He appeared conscious
of the vast superiority of the whites, or rather of
the Americans, to his own race and desired the
elevation of his countrymen by adopting some of
our improvements and customs. For the Spaniards he entertained a strong aversion and dislike; not at all mingled with fear, however, for he
spoke to them always as an equal or superior.
They refused to trade with his nation in arms
and had nothing besides which his people
wanted. Their remarkable disposition to treachery appeared to be perfectly known to the old
chieftain.

After the council, Cordaro desired me to write
a letter for him to his great friend Colonel

Jameson of Natchitoches, and make known to him the manner in which he had remembered his promise to protect the Americans in his country by saving me and my company from death at the hands of his countrymen. I wrote the letter and delivered it to him. On the next day we parted, and I never saw him again. In my trip to the Comanche country in 1824 I was informed by the Indians that he went to Natchitoches with my letter to Colonel Jameson, who gave him three horses, loaded with presents. By this means he returned to his country a rich man, and soon after became sick and died. He was a sagacious, right-hearted patriot and a brave warrior, who in different circumstances might have accomplished the destiny of a hero and savior of his country.

I continued my trading, though without much success on account of the scarcity of money. I had seen enough of Mexican society to be thoroughly disgusted with it. I had not supposed it possible for any society to be as profligate and vicious as I found all ranks of that in Santa Fe. The Indians are much superior to their Spanish masters in all the qualities of a useful and meritorious population.

On the fifth of February a celebration took place of Mexican Independence.[75] A few days be-

[75]H. H. Bancroft (*History of Arizona and New Mexico,* 308–309) has an account of the celebration based upon

fore this appointed time, a meeting of the Spanish officers and principal citizens was held at the house of the Alcalde to make arrangements for the celebration. They sent for me, asked what was the custom in my country on such occasions, and requested my advice in the matter. I advised them to raise a liberty pole, hoist a flag, and fire a salute for each Province. They counted up the provinces or states, and discovered that Mexico contained twenty-one, including Texas. They said they knew nothing of the rule of proceeding in such cases and desired me to superintend the work. I sent out men to the neighboring mountains for the tallest pine that could be found. They returned with one thirty feet long. I sent them out again, and they brought in another much longer than the first. I spliced these together, prepared a flag rope, and raised the whole, as a liberty pole, about seventy feet high.

There was now great perplexity for a national emblem and motto for the flag, none having yet been devised, and those of Spain being out of the question. I recommended the eagle, but they at last agreed upon two clasped hands in sign of brotherhood and amity with all nations. By day-

contemporary reports. The date was January 6, 1822. It seems evident that James' narrative pictures his role in the celebration as much more important than it actually was.

light on the morning of the fifth I was aroused to direct the raising of the flag. I arose and went to the square, where I found about a dozen men with the Governor, Don Facundo Melgares,[76] all in a quandary, not knowing what to do. I informed the Governor that all was ready for raising the flag, which honor belonged to him. "Oh, do it yourself," said he, "you understand such things." So I raised the first flag in the free and independent State of New Mexico. As the flag went up, the cannon fired and men and women from all quarters of the city came running, some half-dressed, to the public square, which was soon filled with the population of this city. The people of the surrounding country also came in, and for five days the square was covered with Spaniards and Indians from every part of the Province.

During this whole time the city exhibited a scene of universal carousing and revelry. All classes abandoned themselves to the most reckless dissipation and profligacy. No Italian car-

[76]Melgares was the last Spanish Governor of New Mexico, serving in this capacity from 1818 to 1822. He was a veteran soldier, and the official who in 1806 received Lieutenant Zebulon M. Pike and conducted him to Chihuahua. Pike was treated by him with utmost courtesy, and parted from him "with the greatest friendship."— See *The Southwestern Expedition of Zebulon M. Pike,* the Lakeside Classics volume for 1925.

nival ever exceeded this celebration in thought-lessness, vice, and licentiousness of every description. Men, women, and children crowded every part of the city, and the carousal was kept up equally by night and day. There seemed to be no time for sleep. Tables for gambling surrounded the square and continually occupied the attention of crowds. Dice and faro-banks were all the time in constant play. I never saw any people so infatuated with the passion for gaming. Women of rank were seen betting at the faro-banks and dice tables. They frequently lost all their money; then followed the jewelry from their fingers, arms, and ears: then the rebozo or sash edged with gold which they wear over the shoulders was staked and lost, when the fair gamesters would go to their homes for money to redeem the last pledge and, if possible, continue the play.

Men and women on all sides of me were thus engaged, and were all equally absorbed in the fluctuating fortunes of these games. The demon of chance and of avarice seemed to possess them all, to the loss of what little reason nature had originally made theirs. One universal jubilee, like bedlam broke loose, reigned in Santa Fe for five days and nights. Freedom without restraint or license was the order of the day; and thus did these rejoicing republicans continue the celebration of their Independence, till nature was too much exhausted to support the dissipation any longer. The crowds then dispersed to their homes with all the punishments of excess with which pleasure visits her votaries.

I saw enough during this five days' revelry to convince me that the republicans of New Mexico were unfit to govern themselves or anybody else. The Indians acted with more moderation and reason in their rejoicing than the Spaniards. On the second day of the celebration a large company of men and women from San Felipe, an Indian town forty miles south of Santa Fe, marched into the city, displaying the best-formed persons I had yet seen in the country.[77] The men were a head taller than the Spaniards around them, and their women were extremely beautiful, with fine figures and a graceful, elegant carriage. They were all tastefully dressed in cotton cloth of their own weaving and decorated with coral beads of a brilliant red color. Many wore rich pearl necklaces and jewelry of great value. I was told by

[77] The pueblo of San Felipe, on the west side of the Rio Grande about thirty miles from Santa Fe, was visited by Coronado in 1541. Lieutenant Pike visited it in 1807, and his report contains an interesting account of the place. He estimated the population at 1000 and was astonished at the erudition of the priest, Father Rubi. In Colonel Wm. H. Emory's *Notes of a Military Reconnoissance . . .*, pp. 38 and 461, are two views of San Felipe as it looked to the American conquerors in September, 1846.

Ortise that the ornaments of stone, silver, and gold which some of these Indian ladies wore were worth five hundred dollars. The red coral was worth one hundred dollars per pound. Many of the Indians, as the reader may suppose from this description of their women, are very wealthy. The men were also elegantly dressed in fine cloth, manufactured by their own wives and daughters. The Americans with their tariff and "protection of home industry," might learn a lesson from these wise and industrious Indians. I heard nothing among them of a tariff to protect their "domestic manufactures." They worked and produced, and protection came of itself without the curse of government interference.

This Indian company danced very gracefully upon the public square to the sound of a drum and the singing of the older members of their band. In this exercise they displayed great skill and dexterity. When intermingled in apparently hopeless confusion in a very complicated figure, so that the dance seemed on the point of breaking up, suddenly at the tap of the drum each found his partner and each couple their place without the least disorder and in admirable harmony. About the same time the Pecos Indians came into the city, dressed in skins of bulls and bears. At a distance their disguise was quite successful and they looked like the animals which they counterfeited so well that the people fled, frightened at their appearance, in great confusion from the square.

I have spoken before in favorable terms of the Mexican Indians. They are a nobler race of people than their masters, the descendants of the conquerors; more courageous and more generous; more faithful to their word and more ingenuous and intellectual than the Spaniards. The men are generally six feet in stature, well formed and of an open, frank, and manly deportment. Their women are very fascinating, and far superior in virtue, as in beauty, to the greater number of the Spanish females. I was informed that all the tribes, the Utahs, the Navahoes, and others inhabiting the country west of the mountains to the Gulf of California, like those in Mexico lived in comfortable houses, raised wheat and corn, and had good mills for grinding their grain.[78] I saw many specimens of their skill in the

[78] James' information concerning the Navahoes was not particularly accurate. A more accurate report is supplied by Col. Wm. H. Emory in his *Notes of a Military Reconnoissance* . . ., 30 Cong. 1 Sess., Exec. Doc. 41, p. 47; "I saw here [near Alberquerque] the hiding places of the Navahoes, who, when few in number, wait for the night to descend upon the valley and carry off the fruit, sheep, women, and children of the Mexicans. When in numbers, they come in daytime and levy their dues. Their retreats and caverns are at a distance to the west [of the Rio Grande] in high and inaccessible mountains, where troops

useful arts, and brought home with me some blankets and counterpanes of Indian manufacture of exquisite workmanship, which I have used in my family for twenty-five years. They are generally far in advance of the Spaniards around them in all the arts of civilized life, as well as in the virtues that give value to national character.

In the latter part of February I received a deputation of fifty Indians from the Utah tribe on

of the United States will find great difficulty in overtaking and subduing them, but where the Mexicans have never thought of penetrating. Few in numbers, disdaining the cultivation of the soil and even the rearing of cattle, they draw all their supplies from the valley of the Del Norte [the Rio Grande] ... They are prudent in their depredations, never taking so much from one man as to ruin him. [Governor] Armijo never permitted the inhabitants to war upon these thieves. The power he had of letting these people loose on the Mexicans was the great secret of his arbitrary sway over a people who hated and despised him. Any offender against Armijo was pretty sure to have a visit from the Navahoes."

At this time (1846) the tribe was supposed to number about 7000 souls. Treaties made in 1846 and in 1849 requiring them to maintain peaceful relations with the United States were ignored by the Navahoes until in 1863 Colonel Kit Carson was ordered to reduce them to submission. He executed the task so thoroughly that hostilities were ended permanently and the Navahoes began the adjustment to a peaceful way of life. Since 1863 their numbers have multiplied approximately ten times. Although their reservation has repeatedly been enlarged, the pressure of ever-increasing numbers upon the resources of a predominantly pastoral economy presents a problem which is seemingly unsolvable.

the west side of the mountains. They came riding into the city and paraded on the public square, all well mounted on the most elegant horses I had ever seen. The animals were of a very superior breed, with their slender tapering legs and short, fine hair, like our best blooded racers. They were of almost every color, some spotted and striped as if painted for ornament. The Indians alighted at the Council House and sent a request for me to visit them. On arriving I found them all awaiting me in the Council House, with a company of Spanish officers and gentlemen led hither by curiosity. On entering I was greeted by the chief and his companions, who shook hands with me. The chief, whose name was Lechat, was a young man of about thirty and of a right princely port and bearing. He told me in the Spanish language, which he spoke fluently, that he had come expressly to see me and have a talk with me. "You are Americans, we are told, and you have come from your country afar off to trade with the Spaniards. We want your trade. Come to our country with your goods. Come and trade with the Utahs. We have horses, mules, and sheep, more than we want. We heard that you wanted beaver skins. The beavers in our country are eating up our corn. All our rivers are full of them. Their dams back up the water in the rivers all along their course from the mountains to the Big Wa-

ter. Come over among us and you shall have as
many beaver skins as you want."

Turning round and pointing to the Spaniards
in most contemptuous manner and with a scorn-
ful look, he said: "What can you get from these?
They have nothing to trade with you. They have
nothing but a few poor horses and mules, a little
puncha, and a little *tola* (tobacco and corn meal
porridge) not fit for any body to use. They are
poor—too poor for you to trade with. Come
among the Utahs if you wish to trade with profit.
Look at our horses here. Have the Spaniards any
such horses? No, they are too poor. Such as
these we have in our country by the thousand,
and also cattle, sheep, and mules. These Spaniards," said he, turning and pointing his finger at
them in a style of contempt which John Randolph
would have envied, "What are they? What have
they? They wont even give us two loads of powder and lead for a beaver skin, and for a good reason. They have not as much as they want themselves. They have nothing that you want. We
have everything that they have, and many things
that they have not."

Here a Spaniard cried out: "You have no
money." Like a true stump orator, the Utah replied, "and you have very little. You are *depicca*."
In other words, you are poor, miserable devils
and we are the true capitalists of the country.

With this and much more of the same purport, he concluded his harangue, which was delivered in the most independent and lordly manner possible. He looked like a king upbraiding his subjects for being poor, when they might be rich, and his whole conduct seemed to me like bearding a wild beast in his den.

The "talk" being had, Lechat produced the *calama* or pipe, and we smoked together in the manner of the Indians. I sent to my store and procured six plugs of tobacco and some handkerchiefs which I presented to him and his company, telling them when they smoked the tobacco with their chiefs to remember the Americans, and treat all who visited their country from mine as they would their own brothers. The council now broke up and the chief, reiterating his invitations to me to visit his country, mounted his noble steed and with his company rode out of the city, singing and displaying the handkerchiefs I had presented them from the ends of their lances as standards.

They departed without the least show of respect for the Spaniards, but rather with a strong demonstration on the part of Lechat of contempt for them. I noticed them at the council inquiring of this chief with considerable interest what the Navahoes were doing, and whether they were preparing to attack the Spanish settlements.

They had been at war with this tribe for several years, and seemed to fear that the Utahs might take part in it as allies of the Navahoes, for which reason they conducted themselves with the utmost respect and forbearance towards Lechat and his band.

What was the immediate cause of this war, I did not learn, but I saw and heard enough of it to enlist my sympathies with the Navahoes. A few days after the visit of the Utahs, I saw a solitary Indian of that tribe crossing the public square in the direction of the Governor's house, and driving before him a fat heifer. He went up to the Governor's door, to whom he sent word that he had a present for him, and was admitted. What followed I learned from Ortise, an old alcalde, with whom I boarded during the time of my stay in Santa Fe. As he entered the room of the Governor, the Navaho prostrated himself on his face. The Governor stepped towards him and with a spurning motion of the foot, which touched the Indian's head, asked him who he was and what he wanted. The poor Indian arose on his knees and said he was a Navaho, and had come to implore peace for his nation. "We are tired of war and we want peace," said he; "our crops are destroyed, our women and children are starving. Oh! give us peace!" The Governor asked the interpreter what he said, and being told, the *Chris-*

tian replied: "Tell him I do not want peace, I want war." With this answer the Indian was dismissed, the Governor keeping his heifer.

The poor fellow came to my store, announced his name and nation, and requested me to go among his tribe and trade. He said the rivers were full of beaver and beaver dams; that they had horses and mules which they would exchange for powder, lead, and tobacco. The Indians are destitute of ammunition and guns, and Spanish laws prohibit all trade with them in these articles. I gave him several plugs of tobacco, a knife, and other small articles, and told him when he went back to his country to smoke my tobacco with his chiefs and tell them if any Americans came to their country to treat them like brothers. He went off with a guard as far as the outposts on the route to his country. But I have no doubt he was murdered by the Spaniards long before reaching his home.

About a week after this, sixteen Navaho chiefs came into the town of St. James, sixty miles below Santa Fe on the Del Norte, and requested the commander of the fort to allow them to pass on to the Governor at Santa Fe, saying that they had come to make peace. The commander invited them into the fort, smoked with them, and made a show of friendship. He had placed a Spaniard on each side of every Indian as they sat and smoked in a circle, and at a signal each Indian was seized by his two Spanish companions and held fast while others despatched them by stabbing each one to the heart. A Spaniard who figured in this butchery showed me his knife, which he said had killed eight of them. Their dead bodies were thrown over the wall of the fort and covered with a little earth in a gully.

A few days afterwards five more of the same nation appeared on the bank of the river opposite the town, and inquired for their countrymen. The Spaniards told them they had gone on to Santa Fe, invited them to come over the river, and said they should be well treated. They crossed, and were murdered in the same manner as the others. There again appeared three Indians on the opposite bank, inquiring for their chiefs. They were decoyed across, taken into the town under the mask of friendship, and also murdered in cold blood. In a few days two more appeared, but could not be induced to cross, when some Spanish horsemen went down the river to intercept them. Perceiving this movement, they fled and no more embassies came in.

The next news that came told of a descent made by the Navahoes in great force, on the settlements in the south, in which they killed all of every age and condition, burned and destroyed all they could not take away with them, and drove away the sheep, cattle, and horses. They came from the south directly towards Santa Fe, sweeping everything before them and leaving the land desolate behind them. They recrossed the Del Norte below Santa Fe and passed to the north, laid bare the country around the town of Taos, and then disappeared with all their booty. While this was going on, Melgares was getting out the militia and putting nearly all the inhabitants under arms, preparatory to an expedition. I was requested to go, but I preferred to be a spectator in such a war.

The militia of Santa Fe, when on parade, beggared all description. Falstaff's company was well equipped and well furnished compared with these troops of Governor Melgares! Such a gang of tatterdemalions I never saw before or since. They were of all colors, with all kinds of dresses and every species of arms. Some were bareheaded, others bare-backed; some had hats without rims or crowns, and some wore coats without skirts; others again wore coats without sleeves. Most of them were armed with bows and arrows. A few had guns that looked as if they had been imported by Cortez, while others had iron hoops fastened to the ends of poles, which passed for lances. The doughty Governor, Facundo Melgares, on foot, in his cloak and chapeau de bras, was reviewing this noble army. He was five feet high, nearly as thick as he was long, and as he waddled from one end of the line to the other I thought of Alexander and Hannibal and Caesar, and how their glories would soon be eclipsed by this hero of Santa Fe. After him followed the Adjutant in his jacket with red cuffs and collar, and with his frog-sticker, called a sword, at his side. He examined the bows and arrows, lances, and other arms of these invincibles. He with the little Governor seemed big with the fate of New Mexico. At last when all was ready the Governor sent them forth to the war and himself went to his dinner. In the meantime where was the enemy—the blood-thirsty Navahoes? They had returned in safety to their own country with all their plunder, and were even then far beyond the reach of Governor Melgares' troop of scarecrows.

In the beginning of March, finding that trade was dull and money very scarce in Santa Fe, I inquired for a better place of business and was advised by Ortise to go to Sonora on the Gulf of California, where gold and silver was more abundant than in New Mexico. I requested him to go with me; he declined going himself but procured his brother, whom I hired, to go as guide for $12 for each mule load. I packed up my goods, and had got ready for the journey when Ortise came in with a gloomy countenance and asked if I had asked permission of the Governor to go to Sonora. I said I had not, and he advised me to see him.

I went to his house, apprehensive of hostility, and found the dignitary walking with a lordly air up and down his piazza. As I approached, he strutted away from me to the opposite end of the gallery without deigning to notice me. I stood and awaited his return, and as he came up, I accosted him politely and said I could not sell my goods in Santa Fe and had called to obtain his permission to go with them to Sonora, where I had understood money was more plenty than in Santa Fe. "You can't go sir," growled His Excellency, and continued his promenade. I followed and asked him why I could not go. He said he had no orders to let me go. I asked him if he had any orders to prevent me. He said no. I then said: "You know that I have a passport from my government, approved by the Spanish minister." "Oh we have nothing to do with the Spanish Government." "But you have something to do with my Government. I shall start for Sonora, and if you arrest or imprison me on my way, my Government shall hear from me."

This appeared to agitate the little grandee and set him to thinking for a moment. He paced to and fro a while, stopped short, and asked how I was going. "With Don Francisco Ortise, as guide." At this he burst into a loud laugh. "Ho,

ho! Don Francisco will go with you, will he?
Well Don Thomas, you can go, but I will send
a party of soldiers with you to the outposts, and
if any Spaniard attempts to go farther with you I
will have him brought back in irons and thrown
into prison. You will have to pass through the
country of the Apaches, and you will be robbed,
perhaps murdered, if you have no Spaniard with
you. Now go, Don Thomas, now go—ha, ha, ha."
I now turned and left him. Ortise, whom I considered my friend, advised me by no means, to
make the attempt to reach Sonora without a
Spanish guide, and I gave up the project. I regarded this the result of a plot to detain me in Santa
Fe till spring, when they knew I was to return,
and would have to sell my goods at any price.

I went on the evening of my interview with the
Governor to the house of a sick lieutenant, where
I found the Adjutant and several other officers.
They asked, with a sly glance at each other, when
I was going to Sonora. "I am not going." "Why
so, we heard you were all ready to start. You
have a passport, have you not?" "Yes," said I,
"but the Governor threatens to imprison any
Spaniard that attempts to go with me. He has
imprisoned all my countrymen that came here
before me, and I suppose if he dared he would
imprison me." Here the sick lieutenant shook my
knee by way of caution, and the Adjutant leaped

up, exclaiming: "If he dared! What do you mean sir, be careful how you talk," and put his hand on the butcher knife at his side, called a sword. I had a dirk at my breast, as good a weapon as his, and facing him I repeated: "Yes, if he dared; but he dares not, nor dare any of you imprison me while I observe your laws. You have robbed and imprisoned all my countrymen heretofore, but my Government will now stop this baseness and cruelty to the Americans. If you violate my rights while I have an American passport my Government will avenge my wrongs on your heads." This appeared to cool the Adjutant, who said we were friends and that he would not tell the Governor. "Tell him or not, as you please," said I.

I wish for the honor of my country, or rather of my Government, that the name of American citizen were a better protection in a foreign country than it is. Ancient Rome and modern England are examples to us in this respect. A subject of the English monarchy in a foreign country is sure that any flagrant violation of his natural rights will be avenged, if necessary, by the whole military and naval power of his country. An Englishman, like an ancient Roman citizen, knows that his Government will look after him and is sure of protection. An American is sure of nothing. His Government may, amid the turmoil of electioneering, demand him from his jailors, but it is much more likely to overlook him entirely as beneath its regard.

The case of Robert McKnight, who returned in April with John, his brother, from Durango, after an imprisonment of ten years, was a remarkable instance of the delinquency of our Government in this particular. His goods had been confiscated and himself and his companions thrown into prison, where they remained ten years, and during the whole time their own Government was sleeping on their wrongs. No notice whatever was taken of them, and when McKnight returned to his country he was equally unsuccessful in seeking redress. "I will go back to Mexico," said he, "swear allegiance to their Government and become a citizen. I have resided the prescribed term of years, and there is a better chance for obtaining justice from the Mexicans, scoundrels as they are, than from my own Government. I will go and recover as a citizen of Mexico what I lost as a citizen of the United States. My own Government refuses to do me justice, and I will renounce it forever. I would not raise a straw in its defense." He accordingly returned to Mexico, where he probably received remuneration for his losses, and where he now lives a citizen of the country.[79]

[79]The career of Robert McKnight has been noted in *Kit Carson's Autobiography*, the Lakeside Classics volume

While in Santa Fe I was a frequent visitor at the house of the parish priest, a very gentlemanly, intelligent man, where I often found an interesting company assembled. I supped at his house on one occasion with sixteen Spanish gentlemen of education, and some of distinction. The conversation happened to turn on the power and condition of the United States, and particularly on the country west of the Mississippi. They said the country west of this river once belonged to them, and agreed that it would some day return to their possession. They said that Spain had ceded it to Bonaparte without their consent, and that it of right belonged to Mexico. They also expressed great dissatisfaction with the line of the Sabine, alleging that it ought to have been and would yet be the Mississippi instead of the former river.

I told them that my countrymen were also dissatisfied with the Sabine as the boundary. "Ah," exclaimed one, "then we shall have little difficulty

for 1935, p. 8. McKnight returned to Mexico in 1824, where he renounced his American citizenship, married in Chihuahua, and spent the remainder of his life. For many years he operated the Santa Rita de Cobra Copper Mines in Grant County, New Mexico, one of his employes for a time being youthful Kit Carson. The father of James Ohio Pattie, whose narrative was published as the Lakeside Classics volume for 1930, worked in the mines for a time. McKnight's operations were finally broken up by the Apaches in 1846, and he died in March of the same year.

in changing it; both sides will be agreed." "Not so fast," said I, "we think the boundary ought to have been the Rio Del Norte." "What!" said they, "the Del Norte; that would take in Santa Fe." "Yes, Seignors," said I, "we claim to the Del Norte." "Never, never—you will never get it, and if it ever comes to a trial of power between Mexico and the States, we will have to the Mississippi. You will be compelled to give it to us." I told them to mark my words and said: "if ever the boundary is changed you will see it go westward and not to the east."

The spring was nearly gone and most of my goods remained unsold. Money was very scarce, and I had little prospect of selling them at any price. I offered them at cost, and at last found a purchaser of most of them in a Spaniard named Pino, who paid me one thousand dollars in cash and an equal sum in horses and mules. He borrowed the money of Francisco Chavez, the father of Antonio, who was murdered in the United States by Mason, Brown, and McDaniel. The last two were convicted of the murder on the testimony of Mason and executed in St. Louis in 1844.[80]

[80]The murder of Chavez in April, 1843, was an incidental consequence of the invasion of New Mexico by the Texan expedition of 1841, whose narration by Geo. W. Kendall was published as the Lakeside Classics vol-

After this trade with Pino I had still on my hands a large quantity of brown and grey cloths which were unsaleable in the Spanish market, blue and other colors being preferred. These cloths I sold to Hugh Glenn, who again honored me with a visit in the latter part of May, stayed with me two weeks, borrowed forty dollars, in addition to the sixty I had already loaned him, and gave me his note for the money and goods, which (the note) I have held to this day. He

---

ume for 1929. The people of Texas, embittered by the failure of the expedition and the sufferings of its members, cried aloud for vengeance, and plans for a new invasion of New Mexico were made. The movement eventuated only in an attempt to waylay and plunder the overland caravans engaged in the trade to Santa Fe and Chihuahua, which by this time was conducted in large part by Mexicans.

Despite the threats of the Texans, in February, 1843 Don Antonio José Chavez left Santa Fe for Independence with but two wagons and five servants, carrying some $10,000 or $12,000 in gold. On April 10, on the Little Arkansas, well within the border of the United States, he was waylaid by a band of fifteen cutthroats professing to be Texas soldiers under command of John McDaniel. Chavez was robbed and murdered, the miscreants casting lots to determine which of them should serve as executioners. Ten of the fifteen who composed the party were arrested, and upon their trial in St. Louis John McDaniel and his brother David were sentenced to death and the others to lesser penalties. The McDaniels were subsequently publicly hung. Data adapted from Ralph E. Twitchell, *The Leading Facts of New Mexico History* (Cedar Rapids, 1912), 83–84.

wanted the goods to sell to his company, who were trapping near Taos, and promised to pay me the money as soon as he reached St. Louis and disposed of his beaver fur. Taking him for a man of honor I treated him as such, to my own loss.

I was now ready to depart for home, having disposed, or got rid rather, of my goods and collected all my debts except one from the Governor. During the winter His Excellency had sent His Excellency's secretary to my store for some samples of cloth. The secretary, after taking these with some shawls for the examination of his master, returned and purchased goods for His Excellency to the sum of eighty-three dollars and told me to charge them to His Excellency. I did so, and on the day before my departure I called at His Excellency's house and found His Excellency looking every inch a Governor, and very pompously pacing the piazza as was the custom of His Excellency. I remarked that I was going home. "Very well," said His Excellency, "you can go;" and walked on. I awaited His Excellency's return and again remarked that I was going home; that I did not expect to return, and would be thankful for the amount of His Excellency's account with me. "I have not a dollar. The Government has not paid me in ten years, and how can I pay my creditors." I offered to take two mules. "I have no more mules than I want myself," said His Excellency. With this I parted forever with Governor Melgares of New Mexico. Ortise told me I could not sue him as he was "the head of the law."[81]

Some time before this I saw a Spaniard who had been imprisoned for more than a year and was then set at liberty. He had just come from the Commandant, whom he asked for the cause of his imprisonment. "You are at liberty now, are you not?" "Yes; but I wish to know why I have been so long deprived of liberty." "You are at liberty now, and that is enough for you to know," said the Commandant, and this was all the satisfaction the poor Spaniard could get.

[81]The contrast between the pictures of Melgares drawn by Pike and by James is difficult to reconcile. In part, perhaps, it is explainable on the ground that Melgares accorded Pike the courtesy due to a fellow army officer while he looked upon James as a mere trader. Yet William Becknell, another Missouri trader who arrived in Santa Fe at about the same time as James, found the Governor exceedingly courteous. "The day after my arrival [Nov. 1, 1821], he recorded, "I accepted an invitation to visit the Governor, whom I found to be well informed and gentlemanly in manners; his demeanor was courteous and friendly. He asked many questions respecting my country, its people, their manner of living, etc.; expressed a desire that the Americans would keep up an intercourse with that country, and said that if any of them wished to emigrate it would give him pleasure to afford them every facility." Mo. Hist. Society, *Colls.*, II, no. 6, pp. 63–64.

The following will illustrate the summary method of administering justice in Santa Fe. There were many American deserters in the city from the fort at Natchitoches, some of whom had lived here sixteen years, and were generally of bad character. Robert McKnight had entrusted one of these, named Finch, with a valuable sword to sell for him. Finch pawned the sword for twelve dollars, and seeing him with money I told McKnight he would never get anything for his sword as Finch was spending the money he had raised on it. "There is no danger," said he, "Finch would not trifle with me." On the next day he demanded his sword or the money from Finch, who refused to give him any satisfaction; whereupon McKnight seized and dashed him about twelve feet, head foremost against a door of the fort. I interfered and saved Finch from any further injury than a severe cut on his head. He then confessed the fact of his having pawned the sword and named the place where it could be found.

McKnight now went before the Alcalde, a stern old Spaniard, who called his officer and handed him his gold-headed cane as a warrant for bringing up Finch, the sword, and the pawnee. They all arrived, Finch with his head tied up in a handkerchief, when the Alcalde took the sword from the Spaniard who had taken it in pledge and asked him if he knew for what purpose Finch had received it. He admitted that Finch told him at the time of pawning it that he had received it to sell. "Then," said the Alcalde, "if you had bought it, though only for five dollars, you could now keep it, but you had no right to take it in pawn;" and thereupon handed the sword to McKnight as the true owner. "But who will pay me my twelve dollars?" said the bailee. "That lies between you and Finch." "And what am I to get for my broken head," said Finch. "I know nothing about that, Finch," said the magistrate, "but if you do not behave yourself better than you have done of late I will drive you out of the Province." So McKnight got his sword and a little revenge without having a bill of costs or lawyer's fee to pay.

Most of my company had been engaged in trapping during my stay in Santa Fe, and some had gone far into the interior of Mexico. Collecting such as remained, and in company with the McKnights, I now, on the first of June 1822, bade adieu forever to the capital of New Mexico, and was perfectly content never to repeat my visit to it or any other part of the country.

CHAPTER V

Return to St. Louis

I STARTED from Santa Fe with Hugh Glenn on his return to Taos, whence he was to go with me to St. Louis. On arriving at the Spanish village of San Domingo, about thirty miles north of Santa Fe and five from the Indian village of St. John,[82] we stopped by invitation at the house of the parish priest, where the principal citizens visited us during the evening. Here I was somewhat astonished to hear Glenn, late at night, tell the

[82]"St. John" was the pueblo of San Juan, which was visited by Lieutenant Pike in March, 1807. Here he was so well fed by the local priest that he had an attack "something like cholera morbus." The priest was an enthusiastic florist and Pike was subjected to a "lecture" of almost two hours on his favorite subject. See *The Southwestern Expedition of Zebulon M. Pike*, the Lakeside Classics volume for 1925, pp. 131-35.

At San Domingo Pike was conducted through the church, from whose flat roof he obtained a delightful view of the village and its surroundings. Oddly enough, "many young girls" chose the moment of Pike's visit to the church to perform their religious devotions. *Ibid*, 146-48. When General Kearny reached New Mexico in 1846 the Indians of San Domingo accorded his party a remarkable welcome; their welcome by the women of the place was no less enthusiastic, but since the Americans knew no Spanish and the ladies no English the conversation was limited to "the artillery of the eyes." Colonel Wm. H. Emory, *Notes of a Military Reconnoissance. . . .*, 37-38.

priest that he wished to be baptised and join the Church. He said in answer to the priest's questions that he had entertained this intention for a long time before coming to this country; that he had endeavored to instruct himself in relation to the tenets of the Church, and produced a Catholic book called the "Pious Guide."

The priest told him to reflect on the subject and pray to the Almighty for light. In the morning Glenn appeared with a very sanctimonious face and repeated his request. The priest questioned him on the Catholic faith and the novice answered very intelligently. It being Sunday they went to the Church to have the ceremony of baptism performed on the new convert. Leroy, one of his company, acted as god-father and the priest procured a very respectable old lady of the place to act as god-mother. The saintly Colonel Glenn looked the very picture of sanctity during the performance of the rite, and he afterwards made a good penny by the operation. The people were very fond of their new convert and showered honors and presents on Colonel Glenn. He was talking of coming back from the States with goods for this market and many of the inhabitants entrusted him with mules and money to make purchases for them, of which they never heard again. Among his religious rewards was a lot of the finest Indian blankets. The Colonel was a great and good man among the people from this time and bore the cross of his religion with edifying humility.

On the next day we reached Taos, a small settlement near the mountains, in a beautiful and fertile valley through which the Rio Grande flows and offers most valuable inducements to the manufacturer by its water power; but none are here found with sufficient enterprise to seize the offer. The country in the hands of the Americans would bloom like a garden, while now it languishes in a state of half wilderness—half cultivation.[83]

[83]Taos, some sixty miles northeast of Santa Fe, comprises two separate towns about three miles apart. The ancient Indian pueblo on a branch of the Taos River, consisting chiefly of two huge several-storied dwellings, was visited by the Spaniards as early as 1540. It was an important center of Indian life and influence, figuring in successive wars and revolts, notably the anti-American rising of 1847 when Governor Charles Bent and other Americans were slain. This was followed by an attack in February upon the adobe-walled church by an American army, when the Indians were defeated and 150 of them killed. Subsequently 15 more were executed.

The other town, founded by the Spaniards before the close of the seventeenth century, has been notable in recent years as the center of a literary and art colony. In the fur trade era Taos was a center of resort for the American trappers known as the "Mountain men." James Ohio Pattie, whose *Personal Narrative* was reprinted as the Lakeside Classics volume for 1930, arrived at Taos about 1824, and Kit Carson, who subsequently made the place his home, in 1826. See his *Autobiography*, the Lakeside Classics volume for 1935.

Leaving Taos with eighty-three horses and mules, with Glenn and his company who had about sixty, we travelled in one day half way over the mountains, stopping at night in the middle of the pass.[84] Here we were overtaken by some Spaniards with a mule load of bread, biscuit, sugar, chocolate, and other delicacies, all sent as a present to the godly Glenn by his god-mother. He took them, I suppose, with pious thankfulness, much as a hog takes the acorns that fall to him from an oak tree—without ever looking up. On my return to St. Louis I heard of Glenn's sneers and ridicule of the clergy of New Mexico. The truth concerning them was bad enough, but I was astonished to hear them villified and abused by the so lately converted Colonel Glenn. He changed his religion more rapidly than his clothes, and made each change a profitable speculation to himself. Such pliability of conscience may serve a temporary purpose to its fortunate possessor, but I have found very few of my countrymen, thank God, so base as to practise hypocrisy to the alarming extent to which this sordid miscreant carried its exercise.

[84]Jacob Fowler's journal supplies contemporary details of the route the party followed. From Taos it led to the nearby mountains and thence up a creek eleven miles to the forks, where camp was made for the night. The further route is summarized by Coues, Fowler's editor, as "over Chico Rico Mesa and thence along Two Butte Creek to the Arkansaw on the Kansas-Colorado border."

On the next day we marched to the foot of the mountain over which we had travelled for about fifty miles with the utmost ease through a regular and even pass with a very gradual ascent half the distance and thence with an equally gradual descent. There are three principal routes over the mountains to New Mexico. One below San Miguel, by which I went to Santa Fe, and which is easily passable for a large army without danger of surprise. The second, through which I was now returning to the States, and the third, a few miles to the north of this last and of Taos, are both excellent passes for travellers and emigrants, but would not admit of an army in the face of an enemy. They are quite narrow and closed in by mountains of a great height and by numerous defiles which in possession of an enemy would present great obstacles to an invading army. McKnight, who came through the northern pass, informed me that it was much better than this, near Taos. These three passes are all of slight elevation and present a gradual ascent and descent for about fifty miles, of no difficulty to the passenger and his teams. The most northern pass will probably become the great outlet of American emigration to California.[85]

At the end of our two days' journey from Taos we encamped at the foot of the mountain near

[85]The famous Raton Pass, on the route leading from Trinidad, Colorado southward toward Santa Fe and Taos.

large piles of stones placed on each side of a ravine or gully. These were in shape like immense
walls, from ten to sixty feet in length, about ten
wide, and from four to six feet in height. They
were the tombs of Comanche Indians who had
been massacred at this place many years before
by the Spaniards. An old man in Santa Fe whom
I employed about my store informed me of the
circumstances of this cold-blooded butchery, in
which he as a Spanish soldier took part. It happened when my informant was about twenty years
of age, which was a few years previous to our
Revolutionary War. According to his account the
Spaniards and Comanches had been at war with
each other for many years with various fortune on
both sides, when the Spanish authorities determined to offer peace to their enemies. For this
purpose they marched with a large army to this
place of tombs and encamped, whence they sent
out heralds to the Comanches with an invitation
to the whole nation to come in and smoke the
pipe of peace and bury the hatchet of war forever.

The unsuspecting Indians came in pursuant to
the invitation, and brought their women and children to the number of several thousand. The
council was held and a solemn treaty formed
which one side hoped and expected would be in-
violate forever. They smoked the pipe of peace
and of brotherhood. Everything betokened last-

ing harmony, and for three days an apparently friendly and cordial intercourse took place between the two powers. During this time the Spaniards insidiously bought up all the bows and arrows and other arms of the Indians at very high prices, and the third day found these simple children of nature stripped of their arms and entirely defenseless in the midst of their treacherous enemies. Then ensued a scene of murder exceeding in atrocity even the celebrated slaughter of Glencoe which occurred in Scotland a few years before this, and under very similar circumstances.[86] The Spaniards, having surrounded the Indians, fell suddenly, at a concerted signal, upon them and killed all without regard to age or sex. The wom-

---

[86]The Massacre of Glencoe in 1692 embittered the relations between Scotland and England for a long period. The Highland chiefs who were opposed to the revolutionary settlement in accordance with which William and Mary became rulers of England and Scotland were given until Dec. 31, 1691 to take the oath of submission to the new rulers. Those who should not do so by this date became liable to the terrors of the law. Alexander MacDonald of Glencoe held out until the last moment, when he presented himself before an official of the Government who was not qualified to administer the oath. Sir John Dalrymple, the Under Secretary of State, determined to make an example of MacDonald and a detachment of soldiery perpetrated the "Massacre" on the night of February 12–13, 1692 under circumstances of revolting treachery. The affair gave rise to a ballad which was included in the school readers in use as recently as the present Editor's boyhood.

en and children clung to their protectors, who would not leave them and could not fight, and thus they were all slaughtered together. The bloody work continued most of the day and the dead were left in large heaps over the ground. The drain or gully between the stone walls ran with blood on this terrible day, as the old Spaniard told me, like a spring freshet.

Not a man, woman, or child was spared, and my informant supposed that the example had deterred all the tribes of Comanches from making war on the people of Santa Fe from that day to this. The citizens of this town may have been exempt from attack, but we have always heard of the incursions of these tribes on the Spanish settlements, and conduct like this of the Spaniards near Taos would, and did, sow deep the seeds of incurable hate which have frequently germinated since in bloody retributions. The countrymen of the slaughtered Indians afterwards erected the stone walls near to which we were now encamped, and which covered a large extent of ground, as tombs and monuments for the dead. Their power was greatly broken by the loss of so many warriors, and the nation was a long time in recovering its former strength.[87]

[87]Jacob Fowler's journal for June 2, 1822, describing the crossing of the mountain, continues: "We found the Rocks very troblesom amongst which we see a great

On the next morning after crossing the mountain we entered the prairies, which were frequently quite broken and uneven. The spurs of the mountains were covered with pine and cedar. Directing our course to the northeast, in four days we struck the Arkansas a considerable distance from its head. On the next day, and the seventh since leaving Taos, Colonel Glenn, who marched in advance of me, sent back a man with the news that the Comanches were ahead. I hastened forward with the McKnights and found Glenn stretched out on his blanket in a cold sweat and shaking with fear as if he had the ague. I asked: "Where are the Indians?" "Oh there they are, hid behind that willow bar." I searched and found nothing, when Glenn again cried out, "Oh there they are," pointing to two men riding towards us on the opposite or north side of the river, and also to a company of about two lodges, or twelve Indians, going from us to the northwest. I soon perceived that the two men first seen were white, and one crossed the river to our company. They were a company of about twelve from Boone's Lick, of whom one was named Cooper, on their way to Santa Fe.[88]

many Indean graves or large Piles of loos [s]tone throne up in Heaps—about dark we got to the feet of the mountain and about one mile farther Camped. . . ."

[88] This was Colonel Benjamin Cooper of Boone's Lick settlement. Cooper had first located here (then the last

Glenn, as much frightened as before, now insisted that the Indians whom we had seen had gone off to bring up their companions to attack us in the night. He had his horses and mules tied together and ordered his company to prepare for action. I determined to allow my horses to separate for grazing, and in looking for a good place for herding them I espied and shot a buffalo under the cliff. This brought up all my company and a part of Glenn's to ascertain the cause of the shot, while Glenn was crying out to them: "Come back, you'll all be killed by the Indians." When I returned to the camp I told him to send some of his men for a part of the buffalo, if he wanted any meat. "No, I want no meat and I will not travel with men so rash as to fire their guns while so near the Indians." In the morning we took up our march, with one of Cooper's party on his return to St. Louis, and with Glenn in advance, who, intent on getting out of danger, soon out-travelled us. About two o'clock one of his men

settlement up the Missouri) in 1808, but since the site of the settlement was still Indian land, he was compelled to remove. Two years later he returned, accompanied by several others and the first marriage was celebrated this same year in the home of Lindsay Carson, father of Kit Carson. Houck, *History of Missouri*, III, 146. In the spring of 1822 Cooper pioneered once more by leading a party of fifteen of his Boone's Lick neighbors (among them two of his nephews) on the expedition to Santa Fe on which James, now returning to Missouri, encountered them.

returned at full speed, calling to us to hurry on—
"here are two thousand Pawnees." On overtaking Glenn I found two Indians, who said the main
army would soon be with them.

I had brought with me from Taos two Mexican
Indians who wished to go to the United States.
Glenn, knowing that the Pawnees were at war
with the Spaniards, said these Mexicans would be
killed on the coming up of the Pawnee army, and
implored us to let them be killed "peaceably"
and not endanger the whole party by any unnecessary resistance. I replied that these Indians were
under my protection and should not be hurt. In
a short time we saw the whole army pouring over
the bend or knoll before us, which for half a mile
was red with them, all afoot except three, and
every man carrying a rope *lasso* or *cabras* in his
hand. Again did Glenn shake as with the ague,
and the cold sweat stood on his face in drops.
"Oh they are coming, they are coming," said he.
One of their three horsemen rode past our band,
then returned and halted at some distance as for
a parley. I told Glenn to get up from the ground
where he was lying and go out to speak with this
Indian. "No, no," said he, "we shall be shot
down if we go out there." The creature's
courage and senses seemed to have left him together. I went out with McKnight, shook hands
with the chiefs, and brought them in among our

men, who spread buffalo skins on the ground for their reception while I prepared the pipe which we smoked together.

The leader of this army was a brother of the head chief of the Pawnee nation, and one of the finest formed and best looking men I have ever seen. He was six feet in height, with large and powerful limbs, a large head with a well developed front, and keen, dark hazel eyes. His manner was dignified and commanding and he evidently possessed the confidence of his tribe. There was something in him that at once drew out my heart towards him and secured my esteem and respect. He was now going, he told me, down to the country of the Comanches, Arapahoes, and other tribes near the Salt Plains to conclude treaties of peace. They had been out ten days from their country and would have passed this place five days before had not this chief been taken sick. He now looked feverish and weak.

After smoking, the whole party of Indians, to the number of one thousand, gathered around us and four of them marched my Mexican friends into the circle and placed them before the chief above mentioned, who was sitting on the ground. All the Indians except this chief declared that these two were Mexicans and therefore their enemies, and many called for their scalps. A Kiowa chief made a violent speech against them. He, understanding the Spanish language, desired them to speak with each other. They remaining silent, he then requested me to make them speak. I appeared not to understand, but said they were my men and under my protection. The Kiowa then walked close to the Mexicans and in a friendly manner and confidential tone he said: "You are Spanish Indians, are you not? You can tell me; I am your friend. You know I am a Kiowa; we are not at war with you. We are friends. You *are* a Spanish Indian are you not?"

The Mexicans looked like condemned criminals during this shower of questions and one of them, looking up and meeting the eye of the Kiowa, slightly nodded an affirmative to the last question. Instantly that chief clapped his hands and exclaimed: "Do you hear that, they acknowledge it—they are Spaniards, these are the men who have been murdering your women and children; kill them—kill them." I placed myself before the Mexicans to defend them and told the Pawnee chiefs they should not be killed, and the older chief cried out: "Come, come, go and get some wood and make fires. Kill some buffaloes and get something to eat." This entirely changed the current. Losing sight of their Mexican enemies, they ran off with a shout in obedience to their chief and scattered over the prairies on my horses, which I loaned them.

Away they went in all directions and soon returned with an abundance of buffalo meat. When they had disappeared, the chief who had so soon dispersed them looked at me with a smile and said, pointing to the two Mexicans: "They are Spanish Indians I know; but they are with you and shall not be hurt. Last winter my brother went to Washington and saw our Great Father there. He said a great many things to my brother and made him a great many presents, and what he said went into his ear, and my brother told it again to me and it went into my ear and down to my heart. Our Great Father told my brother to treat all Americans well who visited his country, and my brother promised the Great Father, in the name of the whole nation, that we would do as he wished us to do towards the Americans. You and your friends are safe. You shall not be hurt."

This chief told me of some of his exploits as a warrior, one of which, then the latest, I will relate. His nation was at war with the Osages and in the fall before he had approached near to one of their largest villages with a war party, too small, however, to risk an attack. He concealed himself and his men behind a large mound in the prairie at some distance from the village, and sent forward eight well-mounted Pawnees to reconnoiter. A large party of Osages gave chase to these eight, who retreated before them to the mound and then separated, four going to the right and four to the left around the mound, and were followed by their enemies, who rushed blindly into the ambuscade. Our hero, the Pawnee, now gave the war whoop and fell upon the Osages, whose jaded horses were unable to carry them out of danger. A hundred of the Osages were killed in the fight, or rather flight, and our hero, the Pawnee chief, felt all the pride and pleasure of a Spartan in relating the triumph of his craft and valor.

We encamped at night in company with the Indians, the chief lying near me, and in the morning nothing had been disturbed. I made presents of tobacco to the Indians and selecting one of my best horses and a Spanish saddle, bridle, and rope, and leading him up to the chief, who had no horse of his own, I presented him with this one and the trappings. The chief appeared ashamed at not having anything to give in return, and said: "If you ever come again to my country, I will have two horses ready for you." I told him to treat all Americans well when visiting his country, and to protect them from their enemies. He appeared greatly affected and at parting embraced me with both arms.

After proceeding about a mile on our way we saw about thirty Indians running towards us and Glenn took another fright, said that these were coming to kill the two Mexicans, and again prayed me to give them up "peaceably." I said "no," and the McKnights swore they would die themselves rather than desert any of their comrades. They, with the rest of my company, formed a circle around the Mexicans, while Glenn and his men hurried forward and I stopped to speak with the advancing Indians. These were a hunting party belonging to the Pawnee army, who had not seen us before, having just returned from hunting, and now came to shake hands with us. They overtook Glenn for the same friendly purpose and then returned in high spirits to their countrymen. Glenn now pushed on in a trot and soon went out of my sight, where he has remained from that day to this. He sold his fur in St. Louis, went to Cincinnati, and cheated me out of his debt to me, as I ought to have expected him to do after his previous cowardice and hypocrisy.

We now kept our course down the Arkansas and on the next day crossed to the north bank of the river. One of my trunks fell into the river in crossing, and some rhubarb dissolving, became mixed with my shirts, journal, invoice, and other papers in the trunk and entirely destroyed them. The writing was obliterated from the papers and my journal which I had kept since leaving home was rendered useless. My memory, which was always very retentive of events and incidents, enables me to supply this loss with sufficient accuracy.

On the third day after parting with the Pawnees we found the prairie strewed with buffalo skeletons, and saw at a distance in a bend of the river a company of men wearing hats. I learned afterwards that this was a company of traders bound for Santa Fe who had been robbed by the Osages.[89] Supposing it to be Glenn's company, I passed on without hailing them and encamped at night in a small grove in the edge of the prairie. We secured the horses and prepared our camp with care against an attack from Indians, who were evidently in our vicinity. One-half of our

[89] William Becknell, a pioneer of the Santa Fe trade, made a successful journey to Taos and Santa Fe in 1821, employing pack-horses. In 1822 he undertook a second venture, this time with wagons, to Santa Fe. Instead, however, of following the former route to the upper waters of the Arkansas, near Dodge City, Kansas, he crossed over to the Cimarron and thence to the Canadian, from which he crossed the mountain pass to San Miguel. This became the standard route of the Santa Fe Trail, to whose establishment Becknell's fame is chiefly due.

The robbing of some of his men by the Osages, to which James alludes, occurred on his second expedition to Santa Fe in the summer of 1822. Colonel A. P. Chouteau, who was in the vicinity, interposed his influence to recover the horses and guns taken, and to restrain the savages from committing further outrages. Becknell's *Journal*, in Mo. Hist. Society's *Colls.*, II, No. 6, 65–66. Apparently it was the same band of Osages to whom James alludes *post*, p. 201–202.

band slept while the rest stood as sentinels. In the morning about an hour before day a sound of violent crying and lamentation was heard, such as is customary with the Indians when bewailing the loss of a near relation. This is usually continued from early dawn till sun-rise, when they end in a sobbing hiccough like that of children after long crying.

A mounted Indian soon after daylight circled around the camp and stopped at a distance of a quarter of a mile. I cried out *Mawhatonga* (Long Knife). The Indian repeated the word interrogatively, *Mawhatonga?* The Indians call the whites Long Knives, from their swords. On my answering *howai* (yes), this Indian came into our camp and informed me that an Osage village was near by, and that Chouteau, Tonish and Pelche, French traders, were with them.[90] I started with the In-

[90] This was Auguste Pierre Chouteau, son of Jean Pierre who is noted *ante*, p. 33. Auguste Chouteau was born in St. Louis, May 9, 1786. He graduated from the U.S. Military Academy at West Point in 1804, and served briefly under General Wilkinson on the southwestern frontier. In 1807 he resigned his commission to devote his remaining life to the career of Indian trader. His principal activities were among the Osages, whom his father had induced to move to the Neosho in northeastern Oklahoma early in the nineteenth century. Near present-day Salina, Mayes County, he built a two-story log house (characterized as a "palace" by one biographer), where he lived the life of a semifeudal baron until his death in 1838. He married at St. Louis in 1814 his cousin, Sophie Labbadie, by

dian for the village and came in view of it on ascending a hill a short way from the camp, where my companion went off at full speed, shouting at the top of his voice, and soon brought out the

whom he reared a family of six children. In addition to his white family he had various Indian consorts and half-breed children, in keeping with the frequent custom of Indian traders. In 1832 he conducted Washington Irving and the English traveler, Charles J. Latrobe, on an extensive tour of the frontier which was productive of a book by Irving and the material portion of another by Latrobe. In 1815 Chouteau, in partnership with Jules De Mun, conducted a trading adventure to the Upper Arkansas, where they were seized by the Spanish authorities, imprisoned at Santa Fe, and their property, valued at $30,000, confiscated.

"Tonish" was Antoine De Hatre of Florissant, who figures in Washington Irving's *Tour of the Prairies* and in Charles J. Latrobe's *The Rambler in North America.* Tonish accompanied Irving and Latrobe on the tour (made from Fort Gibson in 1832) in the capacity of a servant. Irving conceived a great dislike for Tonish, which the latter repaid with studied insolence and contempt for his famous employer. Douglas relates that a granddaughter of Tonish living at Florissant told him that Irving (in his book) had wronged her grandfather. The concurrent testimony of Latrobe and of Henry L. Ellsworth, who as U.S. Commissioner was the leader of the expedition, supports this statement. Although but a servant, Tonish was an exceedingly ingenious person, whose mastery of the arts of frontier existence was well-nigh perfect. See Latrobe's *Rambler* (London, 1835) and Ellsworth's Journal, published at New York in 1937, entitled *Washington Irving on the Prairie.*

Pelche, the other trader mentioned, has not been identified.

whole village with Chouteau and other French traders to meet me. A large company of Indians passed me to meet the company with the horses behind, and by their shouts and tumultuous riding gave my drove a stampede which made the earth shake beneath them.

Chouteau invited me to breakfast with him, assuring me that my horses, which were now out of sight, would be recovered. I partook with him of a dish of coffee, the first I had tasted in twelve months, and of bread and other luxuries of civilization which brought before my mind all the comforts of home to which I had been so long a stranger. After returning from Chouteau's *marquee*, about noon, we discovered that four horses and several articles belonging to me and McKnight and a keg of Chouteau's powder had been stolen by the Indians. Chouteau raged and stormed like a mad man and threatened to abandon the nation forever and stop all the American trade with them unless they produced the stolen articles and abstained from molesting the property of his friends. At last two of the horses were brought up. Chouteau commanded them to return the rest of the missing goods, which, however, could not be found. The conjuror now appeared with his wand lined with bells, which he carried jingling through the village. When he started, Chouteau remarked that the lost goods would certainly be found by him as the Indians had no hope of concealing anything from their medicine man. The wand carried him directly towards the place of concealment, and the thieves to avoid detection soon brought up the goods which they had fortunately found. Two of my horses were lost beyond recovery.

I remained with Chouteau that day till evening and was treated by him and his French companions like a brother. I saw a singular instance of Indian revenge while here, which will illustrate their stern and inflexible sense of wrong. An old Osage was sitting on the ground when a younger Indian with a rope in hand stopped before him and said: "You struck me one blow when I was a boy, I will now return it." The sitting Indian without a murmur bent his head and body forward to receive the justice which awaited him, while the avenger of youthful wrongs drew two large knots in his rope, and after swinging it around his head several times, brought it down with all his weight upon the back of his old enemy. The knots seemed to sink into his back their whole depth. Leaping up in a furious rage, the culprit rushed at the executioner, seized the rope, and endeavored to wrest it from him, claiming one blow in return. As the pain subsided they became friends and thought no more of the old feud. "An eye for an eye and a tooth for a tooth," is strictly their motto. The blow which he had received when a boy had rankled in this Indian's heart for ten or twenty years, and now, having paid it back with interest, he was satisfied and happy.

Their method of curing diseases is very similar to the operations of our animal magnetizers. The conjuror or medicine man has an old cloth, which they suppose possesses the charm and power to restore health. With this magic cloth, assisted by other Indians in the same exercise, he rubs the patient from head to foot in a manner similar to the passes of the magnetizers on their subjects. This is continued until the patient acknowledges himself relieved, or relief is proved to be hopeless.

My company started forward before me and I remained behind till evening with Cunigam for the purpose of finding the two missing horses, which were among the best. Failing in this, I with my companion followed in the track of the company. Before we had gone far a black cloud gathered over our heads, with thunder and lightning in terrific grandeur. We hastened forward till night, when the storm broke upon us in torrents of rain which deluged the earth. We lay in the rain all night, and in the morning the river had risen above the banks and nearly reached our place of sleeping. The marks of the muddy water and leaves were visible in a straight line on my companion as he lay asleep in a gully which the flood had washed without waking him. We saw, a little distance off, our company, encamped on the spot occupied by the Osages the night but one before.

Pursuing our course down the river, we came to the Little Arkansas, which enters the main river from the north, and crossing it, we encamped on its bank which is here very high. The river rose twenty feet during the night from the heavy rains which had just fallen.[91] Here we left the Arkansas, which goes to the south, after making what is called the great northern bend. We travelled to the northeast, the rain falling abundantly, and came to a creek we were unable to cross. We encamped on its bank for that night and the next morning, before starting, some thirty Osages came up with some goods which they had stolen from a party of Santa Fe traders on the Arkansas above, and offered to us for sale. Our refusal to buy incensed them greatly and they

[91]Floods such as this one are characteristic of the rivers of this region. One such freshet at Fort Hays, Kansas, which drowned several soldiers and imperiled Mrs. George A. Custer, is noted in General Custer's *My Life on the Plains*, the Lakeside Classics volume for 1952, pp. 95–96. Here an insignificant "trickle" of water in a ravine surrounding the fort was suddenly transformed into a raging torrent. The Little Arkansas rises in Ellsworth County near the center of Kansas and flows southeastward to its junction with the Arkansas at Wichita.

blustered and bullied around us until we showed
them plainly how little we were affected by their
bravado. One seized a belt of McKnight's, who
wrenched it out of his hands and struck him with
it a tremendous blow over the shoulder.

After these Indians left us, we pursued our
course on the trail of the Osages. The streams
were all full and difficult in crossing, and the
game exceedingly scarce. In ten or twelve days,
after severe suffering for want of food, we reached
the Neosho or Grand River, where we found corn
growing: this was just in the silk without any
grain on the ear. We boiled and ate the cob with
a hearty relish. Soon after this we were hailed by
Indians, who came from the north, and finding
we were whites, approached us in a friendly manner and invited us to their village, two miles distant. They laughed at our last meal and promised
us something better than corn cobs. We fared
well with them on hominy, meat, and bread,
which last was made of flour furnished to them
by Mr. Sibley, the factor at Fiery-Prairie Fort.[92]

[92]Fort Osage, founded by General William Clark in
September, 1808 as the westernmost outpost of American
government. It was located on the south side of the Missouri River near present-day Sibley, about twenty miles
east of Kansas City. Sibley, whose description of the
Saline in Arkansas has already been noted, (*ante*, p. 121)
was the factor or keeper of the U.S. Indian trading house,
at Fort Osage. He subsequently surveyed a road from

After smoking with these friendly Osages we proceeded on our way, and with great difficulty crossed the Neosho, which flowed with the rapidity of a mill race. I hired some Indians to swim our horses and goods, tied up in buffalo skins, across, while we followed, some swimming and others in skin boats towed by men and women in the water. I was ferried over by two women and a man, the former swimming with cords between their teeth attached to the boat and the latter pushing behind, by which means I was safely landed on the shore. Here I found a new party of Indians, who while our party was crossing the river had stolen three of my horses. Continuing our course we crossed a creek on a raft near the White-hair's village,[93] which was deserted, and

Missouri to New Mexico, negotiated a number of treaties with Indian tribes, and with his wife became a founder of Lindenwood College at St. Charles, Missouri.

[93]White Hair's village was on the west side of the Neosho in Neosho County, Kansas, near present-day Shaw. More precisely, it was on Section 16, Township 28, Range 19. See Wm. E. Connelley, *Standard History of Kansas and Kansans* (Chicago, 1918), I, 225. This town was of recent origin, having been settled about the year 1815. Pike visited White Hair, then on the Osage in Missouri, in 1806. Douglas states that he died in 1825 in Vernon County, Missouri, and that his grave was desecrated and his bones carried away by white plunderers. An interesting story concerning his name was related by Timothy Flint in his *Recollections* (Boston, 1826, p. 155). The Chief participated in the defeat of General St. Clair's army in

in the evening of the third day after passing the Neosho, we crossed the Missouri line. Here my brother exclaimed: "Thank God we are once more in the United States."

We encamped for the night and lay down in fancied security, without setting a guard, and in the morning discovered that a large number of the horses and mules had been stolen. We had not seen any Indians for three days, but had been followed by the prowling Osages, who had now effected their design upon us. Thirty-eight of my best horses and mules were missing. We followed the thieves to the White-hair's village and found that they had crossed the creek on our rafts and were now beyond all pursuit. We returned and proceeded on with the remains of my drove. Our next stopping place was Chouteau's trading house on the north side of the Osage River, about six miles from our last, where we found a hospitable reception from the French traders. McKnight and I went to the factory or government store a few miles above on the river where we saw a few Indians, the factor, and an interpreter, who advised me to go or send some persons back to Grand River for my horses, where

western Ohio, Nov. 4, 1791. During the fight he grasped a white soldier by the hair, when to his astonishment the man fled, leaving only his white wig in the warrior's hand. He regarded this as a charmed thing and subsequently wore it attached to his own scalp.

they would probably be found.[94] I hired him and an Indian, for forty dollars, to return with one of my men to recover the stolen property.

In a few days they came back with the news that the thieves had hastened on towards Clermont's village on the Arkansas, where they had probably concealed my chattels.[95] Giving them up for lost, I returned to Chouteau's establishment and endeavored to obtain a skiff for descending the river. Most of my remaining horses were sore

[94]Chouteau's trading house was on the Osage a short distance above the junction with the Little Osage, near the present-day town of Papinsville, Bates County, Mo. A U.S. factory was located at Fort Osage in 1808, upon the first establishment of that post. In the summer of 1821 the factory was removed to a new location on the Osage in the vicinity of Chouteau's trading post. The following year Congress abolished the entire factory system, and along with it the new factory on the Osage. See Wm. W. Graves, *The First Protestant Osage Missions*, 1820–1837 (Oswego, Kansas, 1949), 23, 108, 115. For a comprehensive account of the system of U.S. Government Indian trading houses see M. M. Quaife, *Chicago and the Old Northwest* 1673–1835, (Chicago, 1913) Chap. XIII.

[95]This was the village James had visited on his outward journey as described *ante*, pp. 117–19. Clermont, who was also called the "builder of towns," was reputed to have four wives and thirty-seven children. Although the practice of polygamy was commonplace among the Indians, the accuracy of the latter figure is highly improbable. Nuttall in 1819 (*Journal of Travels . . . in* Thwaites (Ed.), *Early Western Travels*, XIII, 237) characterized Clermont as "shrewd and sagacious, and no way deficient in Indian bravery and cunning."

on the back or jaded so much as to be unable to carry any burdens. We learned from a blacksmith that there was a missionary station on the river a few miles above, where a good skiff which he had made could be procured. The two McKnights, the blacksmith, and myself went up to the station, where we found a small village of about fifty inhabitants, old and young, and a dozen houses.[96]

[96] This was Harmony Mission, established in the summer of 1821 on the north bank of the Osage in Prairie Township, Bates County, Missouri. More precisely, it occupied sections 8, 9, and part of 17 in Prairie Township, T. 38, R. 30. Immediately opposite, on the south side is Halley's Bluff, a rocky formation 100 feet or more in height and extending along the river bank for half a mile. Early in the nineteenth century an onset of religious fervor in New England and the North Atlantic states found expression in the establishment of foreign and domestic missions. In 1817 the United Foreign Missionary Society was formed in New York by representatives of the Congregational, Presbyterian, and Dutch Reformed churches, with the purpose of establishing missions among the Indians. The Federal Government encouraged the project, and in the autumn of 1820 Union Mission was established among the Osages in Mayes County, Oklahoma, 1½ miles west of U.S. Highway 69 and about 5 miles northeast of the town of Mazie, with Rev. Wm. F. Vaill as Superintendent. Here the first school in Oklahoma was opened in September, 1821, and the *Child's Book*, the first book printed in Oklahoma, was published in 1835.

Harmony Mission was established by the Society the same summer of 1821. It marked a determined effort to Christianize and educate the Osages, and to persuade them to adopt an agricultural economy. But slight success was achieved, and in 1836 the Mission was aban-

A fine water mill was going up on the opposite, or south, side of the river.

We found the owners of the skiff, related to them our wants and misfortunes, and requested the privilege of buying their skiff. They doubted if they could spare the skiff. We went down to the river and examined the subject of our negotiation, which was a rough-made article, of the value in St. Louis of about three dollars. "We have no stuff to make another with, should we let this go," said one of the missionaries. "I have some planks," said the blacksmith, "the same as this was made of, that you may have to make another if you wish it. These men," continued he, "have been very unfortunate, and by letting them have the skiff you will do an act of charity. They can't travel without it;" and I told them I would give any reasonable price for the accommodation. "Well," said the missionary, "what would you be willing to give?" "Ten dollars." "Ho, ho!—I couldn't take that for the skiff, even if I could spare it. But we can't let it go, we want it for crossing the river to the mill. I v(e)ow and declare I can't spare it." "I will give you fifteen dollars," said I. "Oh no," whined the philanthropist, "we

doned. A visitor to the site in 1918 reported that the only remains of the Mission were "a large sink hole where the well once was" and some stumps of black locust trees which the missionaries had planted. Data adapted from Wm. W. Graves, *The First Protestant Osage Missions*, 1820–1837.

couldn't take that little, and besides I have no nails to make another with." "I will make nails for you," said the blacksmith, "that need not be in your way," and again the benevolent trader was headed. "But I v(e)ow I dont know how to spare it," said he. I then offered twenty dollars in specie. "Oh no," said the missionary, "the skiff is worth more than that, but I don't think we can spare it;" and here the negotiation ended, my companions protesting that I had offered too much already.

We went up to the village, where they had three half-breed children under instruction, and these were all their pupils or converts whom they were paid by Government to instruct—truly a disinterested company of men. Learning that we had arrived from Mexico, a number of them gathered around us with many questions concerning that country, and one asked if they were not in need of missionaries in that country and whether much good could not be done and many converts made there. Robert McKnight replied, "they would convert you into the calaboose d—nd quick, if you were to go among them; you had better stay here." We left then, shaking the dust of the town from our feet and glad to get rid of the canting sharpers.[97]

[97]The attitude of the missionaries toward the Indians was sharply antagonistic to that of the traders. The former

We returned to the trading post, made a few bark canoes, and proceeded down the river, part of our company being in the canoes and the rest afoot with the horses and goods. At the mouth of the Osage, Rogers, the ferryman, informed us that at the village of Coté Sans Dessein, on the opposite side of the Missouri, I could procure some perogues of the French inhabitants there. I crossed over to the village and purchased a canoe and perogue for sixteen dollars; loaded them with goods, and with the McKnights I hastened forward to St. Louis. The rest of my company, with the horses, joined me soon afterwards. I here heard that Glenn had sold out his fur and gone to Cincinnati. As I remarked before, he has been among the missing to me ever since. His note I will sell for one per cent. on the principal.

I learned on the morning of my arrival at St. Louis that Colonel Graham, the Indian Agent, had just started for the Osage country to pay out

sought to induce them to adopt a settled agricultural way of life, while the latter desired them to continue in their hunting economy. In the present instance, James' antipathy for the missionaries extended even to their manner of speech. They were Yankees, he was a frontiersman of southern antecedents. It is difficult to believe that they were as avaricious as the author pictures them. The skiff which he wished to purchase was an absolute necessity to the establishment, a fact which may explain their refusal to sell it.

annuities to the Osages. The two McKnights pursued and overtook him, gave him a written statement of my losses by that tribe, and claimed compensation, which he undertook to obtain for me. The Osages delivered up twenty-seven of my horses and mules and said that these were all they had taken. The agent took their word for the fact against the written and sworn statements of the McKnights, which could have been corroborated by the oaths of my whole company, and neglected to retain the amount of what they had cost me in Santa Fe, which was forty dollars each, out of the annuities of the Osages, which were then paid in money. He brought on the twenty-seven which he recovered as far as the Osage River in Missouri, where he left them at the house of a man named Rogers, who wrote to inform me in the winter following that they were dying with hunger. Colonel Graham had turned them out to go at large, and when two men whom I sent for them arrived, only sixteen could be found. Four mules which were unable to travel were left, and only twelve horses and mules were brought back; to recover which I expended much more than their value. The agent, Colonel Graham, was greatly culpable in not retaining the whole value of the horses stolen out of the annuities of the Osages. The claim was proved and might and ought to have been secured by him.

In the latter part of July, 1822 I arrived at my home in Monroe County, Illinois, after an absence of fifteen months. I was supposed to be dead by many, and my family were entertaining the most alarming apprehensions for me. The husband and the father only can appreciate the joy and rejoicing which my coming occasioned and the cordial welcome I received. After the hardships, exposures, and wearing anxieties which I had endured for more than a year I needed repose and relaxation, and I hoped to enjoy them for a short time. But in this hope I was disappointed. My creditors swarmed around me like bees, and were as clamorous as a drove of hungry wolves. I had brought from Santa Fe about $2500, the sole proceeds of my stock of $12000 with which I had left St. Louis the year before. This sum I immediately paid on my debts, and offered all my remaining property to my creditors; but they wanted money. The sheriff, the marshal, and constables immediately beset me on every side and seized and sold almost everything of mine that was levyable. I worked and struggled bravely to emerge from this thick cloud of difficulties. I drove a mill and distillery and fattened a drove of hogs, for which I could find no sale. The way was dark before me and I found more real trouble and corroding care in getting out of debt than I had experienced among the savages.

Man in civilized society frequently requires more firmness of mind, constancy, fortitude, and real strength of character than in the most critical and dangerous crisis of a savage state. The poor man, struggling bravely against an accumulation of debt and difficulty, I have always thought, is entitled to more respect than the military chieftain, whose courage is only inflamed by the excitements of war and ambition. Peace has its victories as well as war, and a high state of civilization, as it has stronger temptations to evil and higher though less pressing incitements to exertion, so it requires more energy and determined resolution of mind than any other condition of human existence. Many a brave and true man in the peaceful shades of private life will receive a meed of honor equal to that of

"Great men battling with the storms of fate
And greatly falling with a falling State."

CHAPTER VI

Adventure to the Comanches

SEEING no way of extricating myself from debt by any regular employment at home, I cast about for some other means of self preservation. John McKnight, who was to me a true and faithful friend, went to the mines[98] to obtain for me a lucrative situation, but without success. He then proposed to make another venture among the Comanches and endeavor to obtain from them the fulfilment of Cordaro's promise to remunerate my losses among his countrymen. McKnight was sanguine of success and I fell in with his proposal.

We procured goods in St. Louis on credit to the value of $5500, shipped them on a keel boat, and the two McKnights, John and Robert, with eight men, started with them in the fall of 1822 for the mouth of the Canadian, where I was to meet them in the winter following. I went by land to the place of rendezvous with a company of twelve men, through the towns of Batesville, (now Fredericktown) St. Francisville,[99] and the Cherokee country, and joined McKnight in the latter

[98]The lead mines of Washington County, some fifty miles southwest of St. Louis.

[99]Fredericktown is in Madison County, Missouri, about eighty miles south of St. Louis. Douglas (p. 191) identifies James' St. Francisville as the settlement near St.

part of February. We had five horses with packs and travelled the whole route afoot. McKnight had awaited us about six weeks. We found him with the boat frozen up, about four miles above the Canadian on the north side of the Arkansas and about thirty miles below Barbour's trading house. On going up to Barbour's, McKnight and I found that he had secured the goods which we had *cached* on the island above in my former trip; but that the flour was damaged when he took it down to his house. He was just starting, when we arrived, for New Orleans, with furs and peltry on my keel boat, which I had left with him the year before, and he promised to pay me, on his return, for the boat and goods. I never saw him again: he died on this trip in New Orleans.

The ice being now gone and our boat released, we prepared for ascending the Canadian. Robert McKnight, with most of the men, descended the Arkansas with the boat to enter the Canadian four miles below, while John, who was seldom separated from me, with the horses and a few men crossed the point and awaited them. After joining them we travelled in sight of the boat till we passed the falls about twenty-five miles from the mouth, when we struck into the best farming country I had ever seen; a beautiful land of prai-

François Church, near present-day Greenville, Wayne County, about forty miles south of Fredericktown.

ries and woods in fine proportion. Below the falls we passed a very salt spring. Elk, buffaloes, deer, wild turkeys, and black bears were very abundant, and we fared on the fat of the land. The soil is extremely fertile, judging from the heavy grass of the prairies and the large and valuable timber of the woods, which were composed of walnut, ash, hackberry, spice, pawpaw, and oaks of a very heavy growth and of every species. The Canadian is very crooked and bounded by extensive bottoms.

After travelling five days through this fine region, we struck the North Fork of the Canadian at its mouth. This river, like the other, is exceedingly crooked, and numerous rapids greatly obstruct its navigation. Our ascent was slow and difficult and the boat twice stopped at night within a hundred yards of our encampment of the night before, owing to the irregular course of the stream. Our progress in the boat was at length stopped entirely by a rapid which we could not ascend. We made fast the boat to trees with strong ropes, put our bear and deer skins into it, and buried the heaviest hardware in the ground, where it remains, probably, to this day, as I never returned to its place of concealment. We made three perogues, into which we put our remaining goods, except such as could be packed on the horses, and with them we continued our ascent

of the Canadian North Fork. Game of every kind
known to the country was extremely plenty. We
killed on this and the main river about twenty
black bears, all of which we found in the hollows
of trees, where they had remained in a torpid
state all winter. In one tree four were found, a
she and three yearling cubs, which the men killed
with axes, after felling the tree and stopping up
the top to prevent their escape.

After proceeding with our perogues about ten
days the game became scarce and the company
began to suffer from want of food. We stopped,
and all sallied out to hunt. The first day furnished but one wild turkey. The second and
third days produced nothing more, the turkey
subsisting us all for three days. John McKnight
and I then went about ten miles in search of
game and found a bear's track, but our pursuit
of the bear was unsuccessful. Returning by a different route from that by which we came, we
descried a herd of elk lying down in the prairie.
We crept on our hands and knees in the short
grass to within two hundred yards of them when
one discovered us, leaped up, snorted, and
brought the rest to their feet. I instantly fired and
wounded one, which we found and killed and returned with a part of the meat to our companions, who were feasting on a wild horse. In the
morning, after bringing in the remainder of my

elk we pursued our journey and in a few days the game became plentiful.

We had hitherto travelled through a very fertile and beautiful country, which will in a few years teem with a dense population. The prairies are interspersed with valuable woodland, and will make as fine a farming country as any in the Union.[100] We now reached the vast and sterile prairie west of the Cross Timbers, through the northern end of which we had passed, and we commenced our journey over the boundless plains beyond them.[101] This is the region desig-

[100]The North Canadian almost bisects Oklahoma, running in general southeastwardly from its northwestern corner almost to its eastern border. Oklahoma City, near the geographical center of the State, is on the North Canadian. The passage of a century has amply realized James' prophecy concerning the future development of the area he had been traversing.

[101]The Cross Timbers extended across west central Oklahoma from about the Kansas border southwesterly to the Brazos River in Texas. They are shown on Josiah Gregg's map of the southwestern country in his *Commerce of the Prairies*, reprinted as the Lakeside Classics volume for 1926. They may be seen also on maps 101 and 104 in James T. Adams' (Ed.), *Atlas of American History* (New York, 1943). For George W. Kendall's vivid account of the passage by the Texans through the Cross Timbers in 1841 see his *Narrative of the Texan Santa Fe Expedition*, the Lakeside Classics volume for 1929, Chapter VI: "The immense western prairies are bordered for hundred of miles on the eastern side by a narrow belt of forest land well known to hunters and trappers under the above name. The course of this range is nearly north and

nated on the maps as the Great American Desert, though it is very different from those plains of sand in the Old World which bear that name. A short grass grows here, but no timber except the cottonwood and willows in the bends of the rivers. Our path had before lain through fine groves of oak, walnut, and ash as we issued from one prairie and entered another, but now one vast plain, extending on all sides to the horizon, presented no object to relieve the vision.

We soon discovered trails of Indians and came upon a deserted camp of what seemed a Comanche war party about five hundred strong. As we proceeded, the Indian *signs* increased. We next struck an Osage camp, also deserted, which seemed to have been made a few weeks before by a war party or a horse-stealing party of Osages on

south, with a width ranging from thirty to fifty miles. The growth of timber is principally small, gnarled post oaks and blackjacks, and in many places the traveler will find an almost impenetrable undergrowth of brier and other thorny shrubs ... on the eastern side of the Cross Timbers the country is varied by small prairies and clumps of woodland, while on the western all is a perfect ocean of prairie. The belt, therefore ... appears to be an immense natural hedge dividing the woodlands of the settled portions of the United States from the open prairies which have ever been the home and hunting ground of the red man." Kendall, 139. For the contemporary conception of the Great American Desert see General Custer's *My Life on the Plains*, the Lakeside Classics volume for 1952, Chap. I.

their route northward from a plundering expedition against the Comanches. The country, as we proceeded, became more and more sterile, the grass shorter, and the timber on the river banks smaller and more scarce than before. Travelling on through a country nearly destitute of vegetation, in about ten days after passing the Osage camp we arrived at the place of encampment of an immense Indian force in the summer previous, as we judged from the signs on the ground. The river had now become too shallow to be navigated any farther without great difficulty, even by perogues. Here we stopped and commenced the building of a fort.

One of the men, now a near neighbor of mine, Justus Varnum, had taken a cold, so severe that it affected his hip and back and prevented him from walking. He was conveyed up the river in a perogue for several weeks previous to our stopping, and he had to be carried every night in a blanket from the boat to the fires of the camp and back again to the boats in the morning. One of the men, when we had stopped to build a fort, killed a large rattlesnake with the entire bodies of two prairie dogs, larger than squirrels, contained within the stomach of his snakeship. I advised Varnum to try out the oil of the snake and rub it on his joints as a remedy. He applied the oil as I recommended, and in consequence became so

limber and supple as to render walking painful to
him, when I told him to stop the applications. I
have frequently tried the same remedy for stiff-
ness of the joints and think it might be of service
in rheumatism.

The fort being nearly completed,[102] I proposed
to go out with two men and find the Comanches,
in whose country we then were, and who, we
supposed from *signs* around us, could not be very
distant. John McKnight objected to my going
out, saying that he or I must remain with the men
and superintend the building of the fort, as his
brother Robert could not govern the company.
"You, James," said he, "have a family. I have
none and therefore I can better afford to lose my
life than you. As we cannot both of us go, you
must remain."

[102]Douglas (p. 197) locates this fort in Blaine County,
Oklahoma. Josiah Gregg states that after leaving the trading house of Auguste P. Chouteau (near Purcell in southern Cleveland County) his party traveled eighty miles
along the ridge separating the Canadian from the North
Canadian where it came upon one of the most charming
prairie vales he ever beheld, which in their enthusiasm
they named Spring Valley. This was in 1831. "It was
somewhere along the border of this enchanting vale,"
Gregg continues, "that a little picket fort was erected in
1822 by an unfortunate trader named McKnight, who
was afterwards betrayed and murdered by the faithless
Comanches." *Commerce of the Prairies*, Lakeside Classics
edition, 86–87.

At his urgent solicitation I acquiesced, though unwillingly, in this arrangement and agreed with him in the event of the river's rising before we finished the fort to put the goods in the perogues and ascend the stream a hundred miles, after leaving a letter for him in a certain part of the fort. I wished to get into the heart of the Comanche country with my goods, where I would sooner be able to open a trade with the nation. McKnight departed, according to our arrangement, towards the south, in company with Potter, Ivy, and Clark, the last of whom was an obstinate, disaffected man, and went against the desire of McKnight. He, poor fellow, never returned. He found a soldier's death and a brave man's grave from the hands of the Comanche warriors. He was my friend—faithful and true to me—and I mourned his loss as that of one whose place could never be supplied to me or to society. I learned soon after this the probable circumstances attending his death.

A few days after McKnight left us a heavy rain fell, causing the river to rise, and we thereupon abandoned the fort about half completed and with our perogues and goods ascended about the distance agreed upon, where the low water stopped our farther progress. We encamped and commenced a fort in an excellent position where the timber was abundant.[103] We proceeded in building the fort as expeditiously as possible, and with great labor soon completed it and a trading house, surrounded by stockades and defended by our swivel, which we mounted on wheels in an angle of the fort. Before this, however, Potter and Ivy returned with the news that on the ninth day after their departure they fell in with Comanches and were conducted to one of their principal villages (the bands in camp are called by that name) and that McKnight called a council with their chiefs, but could not, for want of an interpreter, make himself well understood, Potter knowing less of the language than was supposed. McKnight then gave them to understand that he had a good interpreter in Spanish, referring to his brother Robert, and requested leave to return to us for him, in company with one man. The Indians permitted him to start alone and kept the remaining three as hostages. They gave him five days for his journey to our camp and back to them, and he left them with the promise to return on the fifth day.

After his departure, Clark made known to them by signs that McKnight's company had

[103]One hundred miles above the Blaine County site of the first fort would fix the second one on the Beaver Fork of the North Canadian, somewhere in northwestern Oklahoma. We are unable to identify the site with any degree of assurance.

many guns and a cannon. This excited their fears
and they gave evident symptoms of alarm. On the
same day a party of Indians came in, as from a
hunt, and the Americans were told that two
Comanches of their village had just been killed
by Osages. The whole army then decamped and
removed fifteen miles farther south. The three
prisoners heard moaning and lamentation for the
deceased in two lodges during the whole night.
For seven days they kept awaiting McKnight,
when the Indians upbraided them with his failure
and pretended treachery, but permitted Potter
and Ivy to go out for the Spanish interpreter.
They came in, much surprised that McKnight
had not appeared. I instantly conjectured his
fate. A man sent by me down to the unfinished
fort returned with the information that the letter
I had left was still there. Robert McKnight returned with Potter and Ivy to the Comanche village, and here he charged the Indians with the
murder of his brother. His conduct among them
was like a mad man's, storming and raging with
no regard to consequences. At length they were
persuaded, on the assurance that I was at the
fort, to send out forty mounted warriors with
McKnight, while the rest remained as hostages.

On the third day after Robert McKnight went
out, I saw an Indian on a mound, surveying our
encampment. I hoisted the flag and fired the

swivel, when he was soon joined by others, all
splendidly mounted on the best of horses, and I
noticed Robert McKnight on a mule in their
midst, and guarded. They stopped on the hill as
if waiting for a parley with us and I took my pistols, placed a plume in my hat, and went out to
them. McKnight pointed me to their Chief, who
was a Towash,[104] and whom I invited into the
fort. He advanced with his band very cautiously
and when within two hundred yards of the fort

[104]The Towash or Wichita Indians were probably related to the Pawnees, although their tribal history is
obscure. In the nineteenth century they were located on
the Red and Washita rivers, and their name has been left
to the Wichita Mountains of southern Oklahoma. According to Gregg (*Commerce of the Prairies*) they were
chiefly remarkable for the profuse tatooing of their bodies.
In 1834 General Henry Dodge conducted the Mounted
Dragoon Regiment on a campaign from Fort Gibson
among the southwestern tribes whose outward terminus
was reached at the Towash village, then on the north
fork of Red River, a short distance below its junction
with Elm Fork. Dodge apparently regarded them as Pawnees and in his address to them he stated that this was
the first time American officers had ever visited the Pawnees. The Towash were sometimes called Pawnee Picts,
although they bore no relation to the Piqua Indians and
according to some authorities none to the Pawnees. General James' expedition among them in 1823 was very
much a pioneer adventure for an American, although the
tribe had probably had long-established contacts with the
Spanish. The journal of General Dodge's expedition is
printed in *Am. State Papers, Military Affairs*, V, 377. An
extensive account of it is in Grant Foreman's *Pioneer
Days in the Southwest.*

alighted and walked around to the river bank, looking for some traces of the Osages. Finding none, but still suspicious, he entered the fort and examined every nook and corner of it, and then looked at my goods. He appeared satisfied and called to his company, who rode up, but before they would enter the fort they searched up and down the river bank for vestiges of their enemies.

I entertained them with boiled buffalo meat and while they were eating I inquired of Mc-Knight if Big Star was at the village. He said no, and that these were another tribe whom I had not seen before. I remarked to him that I recognised one Indian among them whom I had certainly seen before and had endeavored to hire as an interpreter at the village where we were robbed on my former trip. "His name," said I, "is Whon (from the Spanish, John)." As I mentioned his name the Indian raised his head, looked at me, and instantly cast his eyes on the ground. The Chief asked the interpreter what I had said, and on hearing it asked me where I had seen Whon. When I had told him of our former acquaintance, he and Whon conversed together a moment, when Whon arose and threw his arms around my neck and asked in Spanish how I had been. McKnight asked why he had not spoken to *him* in Spanish, as he spoke it so well. He said he had come to see if I was really the man spoken of by John McKnight, and that he had been commanded not to speak Spanish or let us know who he was. John McKnight had told them as plainly as he could by Potter that I had visited their country the year before, and had now returned because I had promised Cordaro that I would do so, for the purpose of trading with them.

The Chief now told me that the nation would not come to the fort to trade, on account of the Osages, and I agreed to go with them in the morning with goods to their village. McKnight proposed in the night to put all the goods into the boats and escape down the river, as they had undoubtedly killed his brother and might do the same deed upon us all. He was an impulsive, passionate man, with but little cool reflection. His courage in the midst of danger was of the highest order and perfectly unyielding, but he was unfit for a leader or guide in critical situations requiring coolness and presence of mind. I refused to attempt an escape as utterly impracticable, and the height of injustice to the men who were in custody with the Comanches. In the morning I started alone with four mules loaded with goods and escorted by the Indians under Alsarea for the village, where we arrived in the evening and were met by the head chief about two miles from the town. He appeared friendly, and took the goods and deposited them in his lodge. Potter and the other hostages were all in safety and had been well treated. They informed me that my old and formidable enemy, the One-eyed Chief was in the village.

On the next morning I prepared for trading by making presents, according to custom, of knives, tobacco, cloths for breech garments, &c., which, though a large heap when together, made a small appearance when divided among all this band. The trade then began. They claimed twelve articles for a horse. I made four yards of British strouding at $5.50 per yard and two yards of calico at 62½ cents to count three, and a knife, flint, tobacco, looking-glass, and other small articles made up the complement. They brought to me some horses for which I refused the stipulated price. They then produced others which were really fine animals, worth at least $100 each in St. Louis. I bought seventeen of these, but would not take any more at the same price, the rest being inferior. The refusal enraged the Chief, who said I must buy them, and on my persisting in my course, drove away the Indians from around me and left me alone. After a short time he returned with a request that I should buy some buffalo and beaver skins, to which I acceded. He went away and the women soon returned with the fur and skins, of which I bought a much larger quantity than I wished then to have on my hands. The Chief again came up and drove away all my women customers, and I was again left alone with the three who had come with Mc-Knight.

No Indian came near me for the rest of the day, and I sauntered around the village and amused myself as well as I could till night-fall. During this time and most of the night before I had heard moaning, lamentations, and weeping from two lodges on the outskirts of the village, on account of the two Indians, killed, their countrymen said, by Osages, but who undoubtedly met their death from the hands of John McKnight, fighting desperately in his own defense. In the evening the old chief in whose lodge I stayed entered my tent with five old Indians, and all with a grave and solemn air sat themselves down in silence. The Chief, who was a little, low, flat-headed, and simple-looking old man, soon arose, took a pipe which he filled with tobacco, and presented it to each of his companions in succession. He passed me by unnoticed and all regarded me with lowering brows. This I knew portended evil, and I feared the worst. After they had all smoked, the Chief made them a speech in Comanche, which I knew nothing of, and then turned to me and spoke in Spanish fluently. I understood perfectly every word he uttered and heard him with intense interest. He asked when I was going away.

I replied that I was an American and had come from my own country, a great distance, to trade with his people, because I had promised the Chief Cordaro the year before that I would come; that I had done according to my promise and brought them guns, powder, knives, tomahawks, and other things which I knew his people wanted. The Chief replied that they did not want to trade, but wished me to go immediately out of their country. "We are going to the *Nachatoshauwa*, (Red River) and you must leave us." I offered to accompany them. "No, no," said he, "our meat is scarce, the game is scarce; you must not go; away! away! (waving his hand) go out of our country."

I felt that my fate and that of my men rested with this council, and that as they arose friendly or hostile should we live or die the death of John McKnight. This old Chief evidently wished me to start on my way back to the fort, and intended then to pursue me with his warriors and make my scalp and goods the prizes of the race or the spoil of the battle. I concealed all alarm in my demeanor, and reaching back as I sat to a tobacco keg I broke off twelve plugs and took out of a box six wampums, which are strings of long beads, variously colored, and greatly prized by the Indians. I then took out my *calama* or Indian pipe and slowly filled it with tobacco, saying in an undertone and a musing manner, as if speaking to myself as much as to them, "I shall have to go back to my own country after coming all this distance to trade with my red brethren, and when I tell the people of my nation how our red brothers have treated me they will never come into this country. I have brought every thing that my red brothers want for war or for peace, guns and powder and ball and clothes for their women, and now they are driving me out of their country like a spy or a thief, instead of a friend and brother as I am."

When I had lighted the pipe, I presented it with one hand, and the two plugs of tobacco and a wampum with the other, to the Chief, saying to him: "This is better than you can get from the Spaniards." I well knew the sacredness of this offer, and that the Indian dare not offend the Great Spirit by refusing a present of tobacco and wampum, even from his bitterest enemy. The chief hesitated long, but at last slowly raised his hand, took my presents, and smoked the pipe. Giving one puff to the skies, one to the earth, two to the winds and waters on the right and left, and then a few whiffs on his own and our accounts, he returned the pipe to me. In the same manner I presented it to an old Indian who sat beside him, and who kept his head down and his eyes shut. I held the presents close to his face for some time, when the Chief spoke to him and he slowly raised his hand without looking up, took the presents, smelled of the tobacco, pressed it to his heart, and raised his head with a smile.

The white man had gained the ascendant. The scene changed and all was friendly welcome where before was nothing but menacing and frowning coldness. All the others now received my presents and we smoked out the pipe in the friendship and confidence of brothers. The Chief then very earnestly asked me if I had seen the Osages. I said, "I have not, but you know that this is their hunting ground and they may be in the country." They said they knew this, and some further conversation established our intimacy on a firm footing. The Chief then went out into the village and proclaimed in a loud voice that all should prepare to go next morning over to the Canadian to trade with the *Tabbahoes*, their white friends. Before this we were called Americanos, which was a less familiar and friendly appellation than the former. The proclamation was continued by the herald on horseback till late at night, each sentence ending with *Tabbahoes*. "Get up your horses and make ready to go over to the white man's and trade with the *Tabbahoes*. They have come a great way and brought us many good things—the *Tabbahoes* are good." This was loudly sounded before my lodge, and throughout the village all was preparation, joy, and gladness.

About sundown Potter entered our lodge with the greatest alarm depicted on his countenance and gave me a gun barrel which the One-eyed Chief had just thrown down before him and told him to carry to me. This was the last man on earth that I desired to see, for I regarded him as my most deadly and most dangerous enemy, who had probably killed John McKnight and was now seeking my blood. I asked Potter what else he said, and as he answered, "Nothing more," he looked out and exclaimed: "There he is now, sitting on his horse. What shall I say to him?" I walked out to my old enemy and offered my hand. He took it with a steady and piercing look into my very soul. I returned his glance with an air of calm consideration and requested him to alight and enter my lodge. He did so, after delivering his horse to a bystander. In the lodge I motioned to him to be seated on a heap of skins. He sat down in silence and deep gravity. I lighted and smoked out the pipe with him in utter silence and then took a silver gorget or breast-plate, and with a ribbon attached I hung it around his neck and placed two silver arm bands just above the elbows and two upon his wrists. The warrior submitted to all this in passive and abstracted silence, as if unconscious of what I was doing. I then put two plugs of tobacco, a knife, and wampum in his lap, while he preserved the rigid and inflexible appearance of a statue. I again lighted the pipe and smoked with him, when he arose without a word, went out, and rode off with great rapidity.

In the morning all was confusion and busy activity in the village, and one-half of the band started for the fort before me. I followed with the three men, and without a guard. In crossing a creek near the village a horse became entangled and I told the men to hasten on and take care of the goods while I loosened the horse, which I did, and on crossing the creek found sixty men drawn up in two lines on either side, who closed around me as I approached them. I asked the Chief—who was Alsarea, the Towash—what he meant by this conduct. "*Kesh, kesh, kinsable,*" said he, "stop, stop; who knows but you are taking us over to your fort to have us all killed by the Osages?" I asked him if he ever knew me to lie. He said he had not, but he knew that the Spaniards were great liars. "That may be," said I, "but the Americans never lie." "I do not know the Americans," said he, "but I know that the Spaniards are great liars." I then reiterated my bold assertion of American veracity and said: "When your tribe robbed me on the South Fork and I promised to visit your village on the Canadian and trade with you, did I not go as I promised?" "Yes," said the Chief. "And when Cordaro came to see me in Santa Fe, I promised him to go home and return with goods this year to your country. You know this, and have I not performed my promise?" "Yes, you have," he said, and asked if I had not seen Osages.

I told him I had not. With my words he appeared but partially satisfied, and reluctantly proceeded with me under a strong guard, but promised that my mules, horses, and goods should be secured. In this manner I traveled all day, during which time the One-eyed spoke not a word to me. Late in the evening we crossed the Canadian and encamped on the bank. I was marched to the head chief's lodge, where I found the men at liberty and my horses, &c., in good order. I went into the lodge to prepare for passing the night as comfortably as possible and was engaged in looking at my goods when my enemy, the One-eyed, rode up and to my surprise addressed me fluently in the Spanish language. This was the first time he had ever spoken to me. The man who had done me more injury than any other human being, from whose hands I had twice narrowly escaped a bloody death, such, as I had every reason to suppose, McKnight had suffered from him, this man spoke to me kindly and invited me to go with him to his lodge.

Suspecting treachery, I was loath to accept the invitation, and while I was hesitating the old chief came up and called me to him. On hearing what the One-eyed wanted, he told me not to go, because "he is a bad man." Again the One-eyed came to me and repeated his request, which I refused peremptorily, and he walked a few steps away with an impatient, angry air; then suddenly turning around, he fixed his piercing black eye intently upon me, walked up to me, and implored, with a beseeching look and tones, that I should go with him to his lodge. I saw that he was unarmed, while I had two pistols, a tomahawk, and knife in my belt, and could anticipate the first hostile motion from him; also, that we were four men in the midst of three thousand, and entirely at their mercy should they design to do us any injury.

I offered to visit the One-eyed on the following morning. "No, no," said he, "come now—oh! do come—come with me," in a tone of supplication. I, at length, yielded and walked on towards his lodge till the village dogs attacked me so furiously that he was obliged to dismount from his horse to my defense. He then offered me a seat on his horse, in front of him. I mounted behind him as the safest position, when he applied the whip and flew with me to his lodge, which we entered and were received by one of his wives with

smiles and glad welcoming. A wife of the One-
eyed took his horse as he alighted.

In the lodge I took a seat opposite that of the
Chief and facing his arms, which hung over his
bed or cot of buffalo robe. I could thus watch his
motions and foil any murderous design that he
might manifest by shooting him on the spot and
making my escape on his horse. He lighted a
pipe, however, and we smoked till his wife brought
in some buffalo meat, of which we ate, while she
apologized to me very kindly and politely for its
poorness. "We have no marrow to cook with the
meat and the buffaloes are poor. It is the best we
have, and you are welcome," said this charming
squaw. The One-eyed only urged me to eat heart-
ily, and when the repast was over we again
smoked the pipe in silence. Shaking the ashes into his hand, he slowly raised his head, looked
into my face, and asked if I knew him. I replied,
"yes." "Where did you first see me?" "On the
Salt Fork of the Canadian." "Where, the second
time?" "At the village on the Canadian Fork."
"Did you know then that I wanted to kill you?"
"Yes, I knew it." "True, I sought your life, and
but for Big Star, the head chief of the Ampireka
band, I should have killed you and your men. I
knew that you were traders with the Osages; you
had their horses, their ropes, their skins, their
saddles. The Osages had come and taken about

two hundred of our horses, and I went out with a war party to recover them and punish the robbers. We found them and fought a battle with them, in which my brother was killed. My brother was a great warrior, a good hunter, and a good man. I loved my brother."

He then talked in a strain of mournful eulogy of his brother, while the tears coursed down his face, and he ended in violent weeping. Recovering himself, he said that he had gone out on a second expedition to revenge his brother's death, when he overtook me on the Salt Fork of the Canadian and there intended to murder our company. He then put the ashes which he held in his hand on the ground, and taking a handful of earth from the fireplace covered the ashes with it, patting it three times with his hand. Another handful he used in the same manner, and then a third, during which time he moaned and wept violently; so much so that I was uneasy for my own safety in this outbreak of grief. He then looked up with an altered countenance and exclaimed: "There, I have now buried my brother, but I have found another. I will take you for my brother," and in a transport of feeling he embraced me with the words: "My brother, my brother."

He then placed a charm around my neck, which he said would protect me from all enemies.

It had been his brother's, but when going into his last battle with the Osages the owner left it behind with his blanket, and *therefore* was killed. He then asked if the Old Chief had tried to dissuade me from coming to his lodge, and on hearing that he had, he said: "He is an old fool: he does not know whether he will kill you or not, and he wants me to be your enemy so that he may have my assistance should he determine to destroy you. If he dreams a good dream he is pleasant and friendly to you; if a bad one, he is grum and gloomy and wishes me to join him in killing you. He is an old fool. He and his men expect to get back all the horses that you bought of them at the village, and that was the reason of their selling so many of the best to you; but you are now safe, you and your property. They shall not harm you or take back any of the horses. Though my men are few, yet every Indian in the nation fears me. They shall treat you well. I will describe you to all the nation so that whenever you come among us you shall be safe from all danger. I will tell them you are my brother."

We then conversed on various subjects, the battles he had fought, his ideas of religion, &c. He bore proofs of his courage on his person, in five wounds some of them large and dangerous. An arrow had pierced his left eye and a lance his side but owing to the charm, or medicine, which he wore, his enemies had been unable to kill him. He had been christened in the Spanish country, and said: "I believe, as you do, in the Great Spirit. If I do well I shall go to a good place and be happy. If I do badly I shall go to the bad place and be miserable."

On taking leave I requested him to accompany me to keep off the dogs. "Take my horse," said he. "But how shall I return him?" "You will not return him, you will keep him, my brother, keep him in remembrance of me." I left with a lighter heart than I had brought to the lodge of the One-eyed Chief. I counted much on the benefit of his friendship, and subsequent events proved that I did not overrate its advantages. I met the Old Chief on my return, who asked me if I had bought the horse of the One-eyed. His countenance fell on hearing the manner of my acquiring the animal, and he requested me to exchange for a fine spotted war horse of his own, and then offered to give two for that of "my brother's." I refused the insidious proposal, which was intended only to sow dissension between me and my new friend, and the Chief appeared very angry at his failure.

Early the following morning I saw the One-eyed Chief coming with two ribs of buffalo meat, and calling to me "*moneta, moneta*, (my brother) your sister has sent some buffalo meat for your breakfast." The chiefs of the army, who were all present and heard this unexpected salutation, looked at each other in astonishment at this extraordinary treatment of me by their greatest brave, who so lately appeared so implacable in his hostility to me. Their conduct towards me and the men immediately changed. No guard was, after this, kept over us, and we were treated with respect and kindness. My powerful "brother," put a new face on our affairs and very probably saved us from the fate of McKnight. We now proceeded towards the fort, the One-eyed riding by my side and talking very good humoredly and with great animation on a variety of topics.

About the middle of the day I noticed preparations making by the warriors as for battle. I asked the One-eyed what this signified, and before he could reply Alsarea rode up and exclaimed "Osages, Osages, a heap," and asked me whether I would stay, or go over to them. "I will stay," said I. "Will you fight for us?" "I will," said I, and the One-eyed laughed and said they were only wild horses that had caused the alarm. I ascended a mound with him, whence I could observe the manner of catching these animals. In an incredibly short time one hundred were captured and tamed so as to be nearly as subject to their masters as domestic horses reared on a farm. A small party of less than a hundred well-mounted

Indians were in ambush, while a multitude scattered themselves over the prairie in all directions and drove the wild horses to the place where the others were concealed, which was a deep ravine. As soon as the wild drove were sufficiently near, these last rushed among them and every Indian secured his horse with his lasso or noosed rope, which he threw around the neck of the animal and by a sudden turn brought him to the ground and there tied his heels together. This was the work of a few minutes, during which both horses and men were intermingled together in apparently inextricable confusion.

The whole drove was taken at the first onset, except a fine black stud which flew like the wind, pursued by a hundred Indians, and in about two hours was brought back tamed and gentle. He walked close by the Indian who had captured him, and who led him by a rope and wished to sell him to me. I feared his wild look and dilated eye, but his Indian master and protector said he was gentle and gave me the end of the rope with which he led him, when the noble animal immediately came near to me as to a new friend and master. He seemed by his manner to have ratified the transfer and chosen me in preference to the Indian. In twenty-four hours after their capture these horses become tamed and ready for use, and keep near to their owners as their only friends. I could perceive little difference between them and our farm horses.

The Indians use their fleetest horses for catching the wild ones, and throw the *lasso* with great dexterity over their necks, when by turning quickly round and sometimes entangling their feet in the rope they throw them on the ground and then tie their legs together two and two, after which they release the neck from the tightened noose, which in a short time would produce death by strangling. The sport is attended with the wildest excitement and exceeds in interest and enjoyment all other sports of the chase that I ever saw.

A thunder shower now blew up and the army stretched their lodges and encamped. After the shower a war party of about seven hundred men under the command of Alsarea started with me for the fort, where we arrived about sundown. Each Indian was armed with a short gun, a bow and arrows, and a lance; some had pistols and each had two horses, one of which he rode for marching, and one, his war horse, which he led, for the battle. Their appearance was formidable indeed as they approached the fort, and somewhat alarmed the garrison. They encamped for that night outside of the fort and in the morning I made them presents with which they were greatly pleased. At about ten o'clock the whole

Comanche army came in sight, when some of my company were still more alarmed than they had been the day before. Several who before starting talked boastingly of making a razor strap of an Indian's skin now lay in their tents quaking with fear and sweating cold drops. This was the first Indian army they had ever seen, and their courage fast melted away before the spectacle. "Come out," said I to them, "Now is your time to get a razor strap."

The Comanches encamped in front of the fort on a space a mile and a half in length and about half a mile wide, and exhibited a friendly disposition. I traded with them for horses, mules, beaver fur, and buffalo robes. The former I sent as fast as I bought them to a drove about a mile from the village, under charge of three men. On the morning of the third day four Indians, armed, went to the drove and took four of the best horses, in spite of the resistance of the guard, who were intimidated by their violence. I immediately went to my "brother," the One-eyed, and informed him of the robbery. He mounted his horse, with whip in hand, and in about two hours returned with two of the stolen horses. In the afternoon he brought back a third, and at night came up with the fourth. His whip was bloody and his face distorted with rage. He was in a mood to make men tremble before him, when none but the boldest spirits would dare to cross his path or oppose his will. After he had left the last horse with me I heard his voice in every part of the camp, proclaiming what the interpreter told me was a warning for the protection of my property. "Your horses are yours," said he, "to sell or keep as you please; but when you once sell them you cannot take them back. My brother has come from afar to trade with you and brought things that are good for you; and when you have sold him your horses and got your pay, you must not take them back."

After this I was not molested again in a similar manner. The One-eyed Chief spent much of his time in my trading house, and assisted me by his advice and influence over the Indians. He allowed me to judge of the horses for myself, but selected the buffalo robes for me and settled their prices. I bought many more of the latter than I brought back with me, and might have purchased thousands. One plug of tobacco, a knife, and a few strings of beads, in all worth but little more than a dime, bought one of these valuable skins or robes, worth at least five dollars in any of the States.

The Indians had with them a great many young Spaniards as prisoners, one of whom, an excellent interpreter, wished me to purchase him. I offered the price of ten horses for him, but without success. I gave him many presents, which, he said, his masters took from him as soon as they saw them, and he requested me to give him no more, as said he, "It is of no use." He was an intelligent and interesting boy.

The Indians spent much time in drilling and fighting mock battles. Their skill and discipline would have made our militia dragoons blush for their inferiority. They marched and countermarched, charged and retreated, rapidly and in admirable order. Their skill in horsemanship is truly wonderful, and I think is not surpassed by that of the Cossacks or Mamelukes. I frequently put a plug of tobacco on the ground for them to pick up when riding at full speed. A dozen horsemen would start in a line for the prize and if the leader missed it, the second or third was always successful in seizing it, when he took the rear to give the others fair chance in the next race.

There were six Pawnees from the river Platte, among these Comanches, one of whom came to me and said he knew me. "Where did you ever see me?" "At the Osage village," said he, "when you were buying horses." I then recollected that this Pawnee with several others had come into the village to make a treaty. He knew O'Fallon[105]

[105]Benjamin O'Fallon was a son of James O'Fallon of Ireland who came to America before the Revolutionary War, in which he served as surgeon. In 1790 he married

of Council Bluffs very well, and gave me some news of the Upper Missouri and the traders there. He went off and soon returned with several Comanches, and again talked about the Osages and my trading with them. Perceiving his treacherous purpose, I made no reply to his remarks, which were as follows: "I saw you with the Osages; you bought horses of the Osages. Do you know where Osage village is? Is it not here?" marking on the ground the courses of the Arkansas, the Grand, and the Verdigris rivers, and pointing to the place of their enemies' village. At last I told him I knew nothing about the Osages or their villages, which seemed to enrage him greatly, and he re-

Frances, youngest sister of Gen. George Rogers Clark. Two sons, John and Benjamin, were born to this union. John became a captain in the War of 1812 and in 1816 accompanied the force which built and garrisoned Fort Howard at Green Bay, Wisconsin. In 1818 he resigned his commission and settled at St. Louis, where his uncle, William Clark, was Territorial Governor and U.S. Superintendent of Indian Affairs. At St. Louis, O'Fallon became extremely wealthy and through his many benefactions a notable philanthropist. Benjamin, younger brother of John, grew up at St. Louis, under the guardianship of his uncle, Governor Clark. Under the latter's patronage he entered upon the Indian trade, and in 1819 was appointed U.S. Agent for the Upper Missouri, making his headquarters at the Council Bluffs. In 1829 he resigned his agency and returned to St. Louis; he died, Dec. 17, 1842. "Honest and courageous, his bravery reaching the point of fool-hardiness," he was a capable and efficient Indian Agent.

iterated his assertions about having met me among
the hereditary enemies of the Pawnees and Comanches.

Seeing the evil suspicions produced by his talk
among the Indians and the necessity of putting
down the bad report without delay, I went to my
"brother" and told him the Pawnee was setting
his countrymen against me. He immediately
went with me to the head chief's lodge and had
my Pawnee enemy brought before him. Fixing
his dark eye upon him, the One-eyed Chief regarded him a moment in silence and then said:
"We have treated you well ever since you came
among us. You lied to us when you said that you
had seen the 'white haired man' (meaning John
McKnight) at the village of the Osages. And now
you say you have seen my brother, too, among
the Osages. This is all a lie. You are trying to
make mischief between our people and my
brother, and if you say anything more against
him I will drive you out of the nation. You shall
not stay with us." The Pawnee trembled under
this rebuke and walked off in silence, with the
manner of a whipped spaniel. I heard no more
from him.

On one occasion my "brother" asked permission to bring, in the evening, a party of his friends
into the fort to dance, and I consenting to the
proposal, a party of forty, headed by the One-

eyed, entered the fort and danced for several
hours to their own singing and the sound of bells
on a wand carried by their leader. They were
gorgeously attired in the height of Indian fashion
and *bon ton*. They wore eagle and owl feathers,
and were gaudily painted in every conceivable
manner. The One-eyed wore a showy head dress
of feather work, from under which the false hair
fell to the ground. They all danced with wonderful agility and grace, and kept time better than
most dancers in more civilized and fashionable
life. At the close they danced backward out of the
gate, the chief in front driving them with his
wand, and they, in compliment to their host,
feigning reluctance to go. With a loud shout of
pleasure they at last went out together with
regularity and order.

At night we were aroused by shouting and
singing on all sides of the fort and we took our
arms to repel an attack. I saw hundreds of Indians, most of them young men, clambering up the
sides of the fort and trying the doors to get in.
The noise suddenly ceased and in the morning
the One-eyed told me that the young men had
taken the opportunity when the old men were
asleep to improve their acquaintance with me and
to get some presents of tobacco, as the dancing
party had done in the evening before, and that he
had quelled the disturbance and driven them off.

I heard among this party, both here and at the village where I first met them, the sound of moaning and loud wailing in two lodges, from a short time before sun set till dark. I had made a present of a gorget and arm bands to the Chief who befriended me so much on the Salt Fork of the Canadian in my former expedition, and who was now in the village. A young Indian came to me one evening with the gorget and arm bands as a token, and requested me to go and see this chief in his tent. I went with the young man towards the tent whence the sound of weeping was heard, and when within thirty steps the messenger stopped and looked at my feet. I noticed that he was bare-footed. He took off my shoes and with me approached the Chief, who was sitting in front of his lodge with bare feet, like the spectators who were standing deferentially around, and on the ground I saw two women and two girls also bare-footed, and smeared over the heads and faces with mud and ashes. These were the same whose voices I had heard on first entering the Comanche village. They were now rolling on the ground from side to side and weeping violently. Occasionally they scattered ashes over their heads and after short intervals of quiet, arising from exhaustion, they would burst out afresh in irrepressible fits of weeping and sobbing.

The Chief arose, took me aside, and said that I could make these women stop crying. On my inquiring how I could do this, he replied: "By covering them with cloth," meaning calico. I went to the store and got four pieces of calico, with which I returned and covered each with a piece. The chief now spoke to them in his language, and appeared to console them and remonstrated against any further exhibition of grief. Their crying gradually subsided into deep, long drawn sobs and hiccoughs, like those of children after violent weeping. From this night forth I heard their lamentations no more, and a few Indians who had heretofore been cold and distant now became friendly to me. I concluded that McKnight, in fighting for his life, had killed the husbands of the women and fathers of the two girls who were thus lamenting, and that they required a token of friendship from me as an atonement and sign of reconciliation.

The Indians had now discovered their mistake; that in killing McKnight they had destroyed a friend instead of an enemy, and all regarded me more kindly on account of their own injustice to my friend. The One-eyed Chief, who was probably foremost in the murder, had taken me to his heart as his only brother and was now ready to die for me to atone for depriving me of my bosom friend, McKnight—"the white haired *Tabbaho.*"

The Pawnee's tale of having seen McKnight at the Osage village was, I suppose, the reason for dispatching him; and in doing this they had met with a desperate resistance from their victim, who was well armed and a most excellent marksman.

The One-eyed did all in his power to recompense me for his loss. He was my fast friend, and exerted himself to the utmost to advance all my interests and wishes. His wife daily sent to her "brother" some delicacy, such as buffalo tongue, carefully cooked by herself. I began to be reconciled to a savage life and enamored with the simplicity of nature. Here were no debts, no sheriffs or marshals, no hypocrisies or false friendships. With these simple children of the mountains and prairies love and hate are honestly felt and exerted in their full intensity. No half-way passions, no interested feelings govern their attachments to their friends. When once enlisted for or against you, little short of Omnipotence can reverse the Indian's position. He loves and hates with steady persistence and consistency, and generally carries his first feelings regarding you to his grave. His revenge is sure, his love is true and disinterested. You can count upon either with certainty and need entertain no fear of being deceived as to their operations.

A scouting war party on one occasion brought in seven American horses, shod and branded, a tent, a kettle, an axe, and some other articles which I knew must have belonged to a trading party. They brought up the horses to the fort to have the shoes taken off by our blacksmith, when I charged them with the robbery of my countrymen. They denied the charge and said that they had taken this spoil from a party of Osages with whom they had had a battle, and exhibited, in proof of their operations, two scalps as those of their deadly enemies, the Osages. I learned at Barbour's, on my return, that they told me the truth. The Osages had robbed a Santa Fe company and were themselves attacked in the night by a party they knew not of what tribe, who killed two men and robbed them of the booty I have mentioned. It was a fair instance of the biters being bitten, the game played by Prince Hal upon Falstaff, who, after robbing four travellers was attacked by the Prince and plundered of his spoil.

From the warriors of this scouting party we learned that the whole nation of Osages was very near to us, being encamped on the Salt Fork at the distance of about a day's journey, and they advised us to leave our present position for one of more safety. The Comanche chiefs held a council of war, or grand talk, and determined to go out and give battle to their enemies. On the next day they sent all their women and children up the river and went themselves, with their war-riors, towards the Salt Fork in quest of the Osages. When the last of the nation were about going, an Indian came to me and claimed his horse, which another Indian had sold to me without his authority. I was about to give him the horse when the One-eyed came up and inquired into the case, which he decided at once in my favor and told the claimant he must look to the Indian who sold him for his indemnity. Not liking the law of this decision, I paid the Indian for his horse and he went away satisfied and highly pleased.

Before starting, the chiefs in a body came and expressed great friendship for me and regret at leaving me, as they were compelled to do. They said they wanted the American trade, and united in requesting me to encourage my countrymen to visit them with goods and trade with them. Trade with the Spaniards, they said, was unprofitable; they had nothing to give them for their horses except ammunition, and this they refused to sell to the Indians. They wished the Americans to be friendly and intimate with them, and complained bitterly that we supplied their enemies, the Osages, with arms and ammunition with which they made war upon the Comanches. "The Osages," said they, "get their powder, balls, and guns from the Americans, but we can get none, or very few from them; this is wrong, very wrong."

The One-eyed and several other chiefs wished to visit their Great Father, the President, and have a talk with him. They would have offered to accompany me to my "village" to see the Great Father, but, said they, "You cannot defend us from the Osages, the Cherokees, and the Choctaws. These nations are all at war with us, and we should have to go through their country. But tell our Great Father when you go back to your village that we want him to stop these nations from stealing our horses and killing our people, as they have been doing for many years! Tell him to protect us and send his people out to trade with us. We will not hurt his people, but will defend them when they come among us. We will be brothers with the Americans."

The Chief of the Towashes told me that his tribe lived on the headwaters of the Red River and owned sixteen thousand horses which were better than any I had bought of them. Judging from those which his warriors rode, I could believe what he said respecting the quality of their horses. He wished me to visit his tribe and trade with them. Many things did these wild chiefs tell me to say for them to the Great Father when I reached my "village," and all insisted very earnestly that I should return to them in the Fall with goods, and bring the answer of their Great Father and all he said about them. "Then," said they,

"we will go back with you and talk with him face
to face." My "brother" told me to ascend the Red
River in the fall, and I should find the nation not
far from the three big mounds near the head of
that river, by which I suppose he meant some
spurs of the Rocky Mountains. "And when you
reach these mounds," said he, "you will see the
smoke from the grass that we will burn every day
so that you may find us. You can come with but
two men and you shall be safe. I will speak of you
to all the Comanches, and tell them you are my
brother and none will hurt you. You can travel
without fear through all our country. No one will
dare to injure you or take your property."

At parting with the chiefs they all embraced me
most affectionately. My "brother," especially,
showed all the feeling of a real brother. He threw
his arms around my neck and burst into tears.
Alsarea, the Towash, came to me last and sat
down with a grave and serious countenance. He
several times struck his breast and said his heart
was troubled. On my asking him the cause of his
trouble, he said: "When you came here, you had
twenty-three men and now you have but twenty-
two; one is dead. You say he was a good man."
"Yes," said I, "he was a very good man." "You
do not know how he was killed." "No, I do not,
but perhaps I shall know one day." "Many Comanches," said he, "are bad; many Quapaws

are bad; many of the Arapahoes are bad; many
Towashes are bad, and so are many Pawnees.
Some of all these are bad and they all hunt in this
country. They might have killed the white-haired
man. He might have wounded a buffalo and been
killed by him. A rattlesnake might have bit him.
He is dead and you know not how. Here is my
war horse, Checoba. I give him to you. No horse
among the Comanches will catch him. He will
carry you away from every enemy and out of any
danger." With this he led up a splendid black
horse, worthy and fit to have borne a Richard
Cœur De Lion or a Saladin into their greatest
battles. No Arab could ever boast a finer animal
than this; the finest limbed, the best propor-
tioned, the swiftest, and the most beautiful I ever
saw. I brought him home, but before leaving the
wilderness his speed was greatly impaired by the
bite of a rattlesnake.

CHAPTER VII

The Homeward Journey

AFTER parting with these simple children of nature we prepared for our departure homeward. On the next day after packing up the goods we abandoned the fort and began to descend the river in perogues and by land with the horses. Those in the boats, who started before the others with the horses, were to stop at the unfinished fort one hundred miles below and there await them. I travelled by land with the horses and met with no occurrence worth mentioning till the second day. Then commenced a series of misfortunes and unavoidable accidents which continued till I reached the settlements and which destroyed all hope of profit from the adventure, and the consequences of which have weighed upon me to this day with a crushing weight.

As we travelled along the north bank of the river a small herd of buffaloes suddenly rushed out from the river bank on our left before the horses and frightened many of them into a *stampedo*, as the Spaniards call the thundering sound of their stamping, flying hoofs on the prairie. A few of the men rode after them and succeeded in turning them back, but their shouts and use of the whips gave them another fright and they returned into a stampede among the drove, and thus spread the panic among them.

About one hundred ran off at a furious rate on the route of the river by which we had come. Placing the best rider in my company on Checoba, I ordered him to try his best speed and bottom in the pursuit. He started and ran sixteen miles, where he headed the flying horses that had become mingled with a wild drove, and he was driving them all before him and Checoba when a rattlesnake bit the noble animal on the fore foot. Checoba immediately sickened and was brought back with great difficulty. On the following morning his foot and leg were swelled, and he was very lame and weak. I placed him in mud and water, where he stood for several hours, when the swelling subsided and he was much relieved.

By this accident I lost all the horses which ran off in the *stampedo* and Checoba was materially injured for life. I remained till the next morning, when Checoba was able to travel, and I started with him in advance of the company. Soon after crossing a small branch, I saw an Indian about two hundred yards ahead in the prairie, who riding onto a high mound, hailed me with the word *Tabbaho*? As I replied, "yes", I perceived several Indians approaching me from the prairie and my company behind also observed them. McKnight and Adams hastened to reach me before the Indians, who came up friendly and spoke to us in the Spanish language. As we three spoke Spanish they took us for Spaniards and said that they were of the Caddo tribe, who were in alliance with the Comanches. Some of the latter tribe and a number of Towashes were in their party, which they said was on its march behind them. They had just come out of a battle with the Osages, by whom they had been defeated, and were proceeding to tell us of the battle when I observed a party of about two hundred Indians coming towards us and also noticed a small grove a short distance before us.

I ordered my party to hasten forward to this grove and occupy it in advance of the Indians. As they drove the horses forward, the rope which held the pack on a horse which I had brought from home with me got loose and was trod on by the horses behind, which pulled the pack under his belly. He started forward, kicking and pitching until he had got rid of his load, and then returned at full speed among the drove, which broke into another stampede. Off they flew, and many of them ran entirely out of sight on the level prairie, with the speed of birds on the wing. I lost about thirty in this flight.

We reached the grove at the same time with the Indians, who then discovered us to be Ameri-

cans and not Spaniards, which greatly displeased
some. The Chief, however, was friendly. An Indian took up and examined McKnight's gun,
which he had left leaning against a tree, and riding into the crowd brandished it over his head,
exclaiming that we had stolen the horses; that
they ought to take them from us and kill us. The
old Chief ordered him to be silent, and he said if
they would not kill us he would go and bring
men who would do so, and started off in a gallop
towards the Canadian with McKnight's gun.
Many of the Indians charged us with having
stolen Checoba from Alsarea the Towash, and
seemed to believe the charge and to consider us
thieves who had been preying upon their countrymen. One who appeared to be the most blood-
thirsty shot an arrow into the side of one of their
own horses near the lights. The horse bounded
forward and fell dead. This act excited them to
the highest pitch and the old Chief had great difficulty in protecting us from an attack. By an
harangue and a decisive course he at length as-
suaged their animosity and excitement. Their
late defeat by the Osages had embittered their
minds and pre-disposed them to view us with
suspicion. Seven men among them carried
wounds received in the late battle, and by request of the Chief I dressed these wounds with
salve and sticking plaster.

While I was thus engaged, I sent the men forward a short distance, when they awaited me with their rifles ready to return the fire of the Indians. But they parted with us peaceably, and the Chief with great cordiality entreated me to return to his country and trade with his tribe. "We want," said he, "the friendship and trade of the Americans." I always observed that the most sagacious and far-seeing of the Comanche chieftains sincerely desired the friendship and alliance of the Americans. A proper course towards them will make them our fast friends and most valuable allies. An opposite one will render them most deadly and dangerous enemies, and especially so in the event of a war with England. A course of justice, fairness, and liberality is the only judicious one, and in dealing with them the greatest tact and much knowledge of Indian character is requisite for success in gaining their confidence and securing their lasting esteem and friendship. The Pawnees and all the tribes west of the Osages, called by the national name of Comanches, are all of the same original tribe, though bearing various names, and all speak the same language. They are in the strictest alliance with each other and could probably muster a force of forty or fifty thousand warriors at the time I was among them. The United States should provide against the consequences of their hostility.

After parting from the Caddo chief I sent the company with the horses forward, and remained behind with McKnight to watch against pursuit by the Indians. Finding that we were not followed, we hastened on and overtook the rest of the company and all reached the unfinished fort in the afternoon, where we found the perogues and swivel in charge of the men who had brought them down the river and were awaiting us according to arrangement. We travelled on in company till nightfall, when the land party crossed the river at a bend and encamped with the others in a grove. We carefully secured our horses. On the following morning as we issued from the timber into the prairie a dead buffalo cow was seen with her calf standing near her. We soon saw another cow, lately killed by a party evidently in pursuit of us. We travelled in company with the perogues, that we might have the benefit of the swivel in case of an attack.

In the Cross Timbers, which we reached in four or five days after leaving the last-mentioned fort, we again parted company with the perogues and struck out into the prairie. Here we soon afterwards observed a herd of buffaloes running rapidly with their tongues hanging out of their mouths, and also eight Indians mounted, who did not perceive us. In three days we passed the Cross Timbers and reached the long-grass prairies on the east of them. Here the horse flies were so numerous and ravenous as nearly to destroy the horses, which were frequently covered entirely by them. Many of the horses died and all were wasting away under the inflictions of these venomous insects. To avoid them, we travelled only by night and slept by day. I took the direction by guess and in eight days, or rather nights, we struck the Arkansas just five miles below the three forks, where Fort Gibson now stands, and the point which I was aiming to reach.

I went up to the forks where Barbour's trading establishment was then situated and there obtained a canoe. Barbour, I afterwards learned, had died in New Orleans, whither he started with my keel boat on my outward trip. We travelled down the Arkansas to the mouth of the Canadian, and found the rest of my company with the perogues awaiting us at the salt works. Here I took an account of my stock and found that out of three hundred and twenty-three horses and mules which I had purchased of the Indians and started with for home, I had lost by flies and *stampedos* just two hundred and fifty-three, leaving but seventy-one now in my possession. These I allowed to rest one day and on the next day lost five of them by a disease called the feresy, which causes a swelling of the breast and belly and generally terminates fatally. On the day and night following, eight or ten more of the horses died and about twenty were sick with the disease.

I was too anxious for my family and too desirous of seeing them to delay my departure any longer. Here, at the mouth of the Illinois River, a branch of the Arkansas and near the mouth of the Canadian, I left the few horses and mules remaining and the perogue containing the skins and robes in charge of Adams & Denison. I never saw them again and lost all—horses and mules, beaver skins, and buffalo robes. I returned home with five horses just the same number I had started out with. Most of them died, and those that lived were never accounted for to me. The skins and robes were sold by James Adams, at Eau Post in Arkansas, on the river of that name, and the whole proceeds, amounting to a large sum of my money, were embezzled by him, the said Adams. He had been employed by McKnight and was unknown to me.

In every respect, pecuniarily and otherwise, this was a most unfortunate venture. I lost by it my best and dearest friend, John McKnight, and all the money I had invested in it with the vain hope of being thereby set free from debt and made an independent man. The object was a great one, and the risk proportionably great. I lost all that I had set upon the stake and was still more deeply involved than before. A dreary future lay ahead, but I determined to meet and struggle with it like a man.

Leaving the river, in company with twelve men, some afoot and some with horses, we directed our course for the Cherokee country. We found no game, and for several days all suffered severely from hunger. We at length approached the Cherokee settlements, and I went forward alone, promising the men to have a meal prepared for them at the house of John Rogers, a half-breed Cherokee chief.[106] When in sight of his place I met Rogers and told him I wanted breakfast for myself and twelve men; that I had been among the Comanches trading, and that my company was coming up nearly starved. He replied that his tribe had been at war that year with the Osages and had raised but a small crop, and that he had to pay one dollar per bushel for his bread. "But," said he, "I will get you something to eat," and entering his house, requested his wife to prepare breakfast for twelve men, and with a smile,

---

[106]John Rogers, chief of the western Cherokees, was a mixed-blood. James Hildreth, in 1834, described him as "immensely rich," the owner of a large tract of land and of so many cattle that he could not count them, besides huge numbers of pigs and poultry. He was a half-brother of Tiana, the Cherokee wife of Sam Houston. In 1838 Rogers sold 300 acres of land to the Government to serve as the site of the new Fort Smith.

"twelve hungry men at that." I noticed in his house, all the usual furniture of our best farmers, and he was evidently living well and comfortably. The men came up, and by their rough exteriors, long beards and hair, lantern jaws, and lank bodies they strongly impressed me with the idea of a gang of famished wolves. They glared at Mrs. Rogers while she was getting their breakfast like so many cannibals, and had she not been very quick in appeasing their appetites I cannot swear but that they would have eaten her up. She, the good woman, squaw though she was, exerted herself in our behalf like an angel of mercy, and in a miraculously short time she set before us a noble meal of bacon, eggs, corn bread, milk and coffee. There was enough for us all and we arose filled, leaving some on the table, not from politeness but from inability to eat any more. "Well, Mr. Rogers," said I, "what shall I pay you for our breakfast?" "What," said he, laughing, "would be the use of charging men who have just come out of the woods and cannot possibly have any money?" "No," said I, "I am not begging my way. I will pay you with goods that I have." I then drew out my stock and sold him twelve dollars' worth, after paying for our meal.

The father and sister of Rogers now came in and talked with us some time. The father, who was a white man, said that his son John killed the first Indian at the battle of the Horse-shoe, where both served on the side of the Americans under Jackson.[107] "The Creeks," said he, "always fight till death. It takes one Cherokee for every Creek, and of the whites a little more than one for one." Both father and son spoke in the highest terms of General Jackson, as a man, a soldier, and a commander.

I requested provisions to subsist us till we could get a supply, and obtained from him sufficient to carry us to Matthew Lyon's trading house at the Spadra. Below this is a large missionary station,[108] which we were informed was well sup-

[107]The battle of Horseshoe Bend on the Tallapoosa River in Alabama was fought March 27, 1814. General Jackson with 2000 troops attacked the Creeks, 800 strong, who were strongly entrenched. The Creeks stubbornly refused to surrender and all but about 50 were killed. The white loss was 49 dead and 157 wounded. The battle permanently destroyed the military power of the Creeks.

[108]The American Board of Commissioners for Foreign Missions was organized in 1810 and two years later was incorporated, with its headquarters in Boston. In 1826 the United Foreign Missionary Society (noted *ante*, p. 206) was merged with it. The general objective of the two groups was the establishment of missions among the Cherokees and other tribes of the Southwest. The American Board moved first, by establishing the Dwight Mission (named for President Timothy Dwight of Yale College) in 1820. It was located on the west side of Illinois River, about four miles above its junction with the Arkansas, in Pope County, Arkansas, a short distance west

plied with flour and meat, of which a boat load for their use had lately arrived. "If you find the missionaries in good humor," said Mrs. Rogers, "and do not go on the Lord's Day, you will be able to get some provisions, but not without. I was down at the station last week on Saturday and stayed over Sunday. A Cherokee woman came in on Sunday from Piney, twenty miles above on the river, with some chickens to buy some sugar and coffee for a poor woman who had been lately confined. I interpreted for the woman, and went to Brother Vaill and told him what the woman wanted. I don't deal with the females, said he; you must go to Sister ————. We went to the sister that Brother Vaill had named, and she told me that they neither bought nor sold on the Lord's Day. "Then take the chickens as a gift," said I, "and give the woman what she wants." "We neither give nor take on the Lord's Day," said she, and the poor woman had to go back with her chickens, and so I advise you not to go to the missionaries on the Lord's Day."

of present-day Russellville. A roadside marker on U.S. Highway 64 now commemorates the Mission. As with Harmony Mission among the Osages, Dwight Mission was a considerable establishment. In 1829 the Mission was removed to Sequoyah County, Oklahoma. An historical marker west of Sallisaw on U.S. Highway 64 states that the Mission site was at Nicksville Post Office. Graves, in *First Protestant Osage Missions*, 220, identifies it as about three miles south of Marble City.

I could hardly believe that bigotry and fanaticism could go so far as this until I found by experience, when I reached the station, that their meanness was fully equal to all I had heard. We left the hospitable house of the Cherokee chief with many thanks and proceeded on our way. At a short distance from the Spadra I was riding alone in advance of the company when I met a gentlemanly and intelligent half-breed Cherokee, of whom I inquired if I could procure provisions at that place. He said I could not, but invited me to alight and take breakfast with him. "There are too many of us," said I, "twelve besides myself." This did not daunt him, and he immediately extended his invitation to all, and the whole company accordingly entered his house and partook of an excellent breakfast, such as that which his brother had furnished us two days before. This man was James, the brother of John Rogers, and lived like him in comfort and elegance. His wife was a handsome half-breed, whom I presented with some articles of dress, against the wish of her husband, who refused all pay for our breakfast. He purchased of me goods to the amount of fifteen dollars and paid me the money for them.

We passed the Spadra that morning, where I saw the grave of Matthew Lyon, a man who made a considerable figure in politics in the Alien and Sedition times of John Adams. "After life's fitful fever he sleeps well." At Piney I saw a number of Indians, and inquired of them for provisions. "We are hungry," said I, "and have nothing to eat." A negro woman said they were starving themselves and could not help us to anything. I told the man we should be compelled to fast until we reached Webber's[109] or the missionaries. An old Indian who stood behind me during this colloquy caught hold of my arm as I started on and with a sharp inquiring look into my eyes exclaimed: "Nothing! nothing to eat?" "Nothing at all," said I. "Come with me," said he. I followed him about one hundred yards up the bank of a creek, where he turned up a hollow and entered a cabin under the brow of a hill; going to the chimney he took from within it a stick holding three pieces of bacon and gave me two of them. I offered him money. "No," said he, "I take no money, but when you meet a hungry Cherokee share with him whatever you have, as I have shared with you."

[109]Walter Webber, a mixed-blood Cherokee chief, lived near the mouth of Illinois Creek in Pope County, Arkansas. Nuttall, who visited him in 1819, described him as "a metif, who acts as an Indian trader, is also a chief of the nation, and lives in ease and affluence, possessing a decently furnished and well provided house, several negro slaves, a large, well cleaned and well fenced farm; both himself and his nephew, read, write and speak English." Thwaites (Ed.) *Early Western Travels*, XIII, 181. The village of Webber's Falls, Oklahoma, near where he subsequently had a trading post, is named for him.

Such conduct as this, thought I, is practical Christianity, call it by what name you please. Parting with this warm-hearted Indian, we hastened on towards the missionary station, which we reached the next day. This was situated on the north side of the river and was composed of about one hundred persons, old and young, who occupied some twenty buildings arranged in a square. Here we hoped to obtain a full supply of provisions, being informed that one hundred barrels of pork and one hundred and fifty barrels of flour had lately arrived for the use of the missionaries and their families. Entering the town I inquired for and found the head of the concern, named Vaill[110], laid before him our destitute condition and misfortunes in the Comanche coun-

[110]Rev. William Vaill, born in 1783, was a native of Connecticut and a graduate of Yale College in 1806. He was superintendent of Union Mission among the Osages, located on the west side of Neosho River about five miles northeast of the town of Mazie, Oklahoma. Vaill arrived at the Mission on Feb. 18, 1821 and served as superintendent until its abandonment in September, 1834. No confirmation of his presence at Dwight Mission has been found, and it seems probable that James, who may have encountered him at Union Mission in Oklahoma on his visit to the Osage town during his outward journey to Santa Fe in 1821, in old age may have mistakenly attributed the meeting to Dwight Mission. Upon the abandonment of Union Mission Vaill engaged in Home Missionary work in Illinois, where he died in 1865. Graves, *First Protestant Osage Missions*, 243.

try, and asked him for provisions enough to last us to the settlements on the Little Red, seventy miles below. "Well," said he, "I will speak to Brother such a one about it," and went away for that purpose. Another man soon came up and asked me how much we wanted. I replied, "About one hundred pounds of flour and fifty of pork." "Well I vow and declare, I don't know how we shall be able to spare it; how much would you be willing to give?" "Any reasonable price," said I; "What do you ask? We are suffering from hunger and must have provisions."

He left me, saying he would see Brother Vaill about it and I waited an hour without seeing either of them. I then searched out Brother Vaill and repeated my request for provisions. He vowed and declared that he did not think they had more than enough "to do them the year round." I then asked for one-half the quantity I had named before. "We have a very large family, and if we should get out we could not get any more from the settlements." I said that what little we wanted would not make more than one meal for his family, and he could easily procure a new supply to prevent any suffering. "Well," said he, "what would you be willing to give?" "Set your own price on your property," said I, "and I will give it, as I cannot do without provisions." He then went away, saying he would see the others, naming them.

Robert McKnight now came from the blacksmith's shop, where he had got his mule shod on the fore feet and had been charged for that service the sum of two dollars. We concluded that they knew the price of horseshoes, if not of flour and pork. Again I sought out the "brethren," Vaill and the other, reiterated to them our wants, and requested relief as before: the eternal question was again put, "What would you be willing to give?" "Anything that you choose to ask," said I. "We do not think we can spare any provisions," said one. They were waiting for a bid and I determined not to huckster with the canting hypocrites, nor gratify them by paying an outrageously exorbitant price, which they were expecting to get from my necessities.

Without further parley I left them and went up to the bakery of the station, where some of my company were trying to get some bread. I offered to pay for whatever they could sell. "No, we can't sell anything without Brother Vaill's permission." I offered to buy two or three bushels of fragments of bread, which I noticed on the table in a corner. "We use them in soups and for puddings and do not waste anything." My men were now furious and ready to take possession of the bakery and divide it out among them. With great difficulty I restrained them from this act. I told them they would render us all infamous in the settlements as robbers of missionaries, those holy men of God; that we should be regarded with horror by all, wherever we went, if we preyed upon these lamb-like and charitable Christians. I told them we must go on and trust to Providence. "What!" said McKnight, "travel on without provisions when there are plenty of them here. I will have some if need be by force."

I at length prevailed on them to start without committing any depredation. When leaving the town, I saw Vaill at a distance, rode up to him and asked: "What are you doing here?" "We are instructing the Indians in the Christian religion." "I think," said I, "you might learn some of the principles of your religion from the Indians themselves. An old Cherokee yesterday gave me two out of three pieces of meat which he had, and refused pay for them in money. He told me to do the same by a Cherokee should I meet one in want. Here you are afraid to put a price on your flour and meat for fear of not charging enough. You wish me to name an exorbitant price. You wish to make the most out of me, and you shall make nothing." He was saying that charity began at home, he must provide for his own household, and so forth, as I left him in disgust with his meanness and hypocrisy. We now left the river and bore eastwardly, and that evening killed a turkey, upon which we lived two days and a half, when we reached Little Red River, where we procured an excellent dinner and a supply of food from a settler whose name I forget. This was the first meal we had eaten, sufficient to break our fasts, since we had left James Rogers' house, five days before.

From this place I hastened home without any occurrence of note. My family was sick when I arrived, and my creditors soon became more clamorous than ever. Each endeavored to anticipate the others, and the executive officers of all the courts, from the United States District Court down to those of justices of the peace, swarmed around me like insects in August. I gave up all my property, even the beds upon which my children were born, and after all was sold, though the officers supposed there was enough to satisfy the judgments against me, there yet remained a large amount still due. The whole is now paid. In the twenty years which have intervened, I discharged all my debts on account of these two expeditions, of which the narration is now closed. I lost by them about the sum of twelve thousand dollars, and after all the hardships I had endured found myself poorer than ever.

The reader has been told how I incurred these losses, most of which were, perhaps, under the circumstances, to have been expected. I was the first American that ever went among the Comanches for the purpose of trading. Before my first trip among them their name was unknown to our people. The Americans called them Pawnees and knew them only by that name. They were then wilder and more ignorant of our power than now, when they have probably learned that we do not all live in one village, and derived from their kindred tribe, the Pawnees, and other neighbors, a tolerably correct idea of our strength and numbers. Traders would now run very little risk of the robberies which I suffered from them, and probably none at all of being killed in time of peace. The trade would now be profitable; equally so as when I was among them, and from the greater cheapness of goods a greater profit could be made, while the dangers would be far less. Were it not for advancing age I should repeat the adventures, notwithstanding their unfortunate issues heretofore.

Age, however, forbids any further attempts to retrieve my fortune in this manner. I have been enabled through the real friendship of a brother to support my family and give my children the rudiments and foundation of an education; which, though not such as I would have given them had better fortune attended me, is sufficient, if properly improved, to enable them to go through the world with honor and usefulness. I have uniformly endeavored to instill in their minds principles of integrity and republicanism;

and for myself, to bequeath, as the richest in-
heritance I could leave them, a good example and
an unsullied name. With strong bodies and habits of labor, with honor and intelligence, they
will succeed in a country of liberty and equal
rights to all.

I have always been true to my country, and
uniformly studied to advance the interests of my
countrymen in all my transactions with the savages and Spaniards; and I have my reward in the
satisfaction derived from a consciousness and patriotic discharge of duty on all occasions. At the
age of sixty-three, with broken health, I feel none
of the peevishness of age. I look forward cheerfully and hopefully on the coming days, without

"Shuddering to feel their shadows o'er me creep,"

and rejoice, in my decline, over the rise and glori-
ous prospects of my country. I have the consola-
tion of being able to recall to my mind several
manifestations of the confidence and esteem of
my fellow-citizens, exerted towards me at a time
when the hand of misfortune bore heaviest upon
my head. They did me the honor in eighteen
hundred and twenty-five of electing me General
of the Second Brigade, First Division of the
Militia of Illinois, an office which I now hold. I
was also elected, in the same year, to represent
the county of Monroe in the Legislature of Illi-

nois, of which I was a member for two sessions. I was appointed Post Master in the same county in eighteen hundred and twenty-seven and have held the appointment ever since. I would mention my agency in the Black Hawk War of eighteen hundred and thirty-two, in which I served as Major, were it not a war in which no honor was gained by anyone, and the history of which, for the credit of the country, ought never to be written.

These proofs of the esteem of my countrymen are gratifying and consoling amidst the difficulties which have so long weighed me down, and are evidence that a generous people will appreciate the intrinsic character of a man, independent of adventitious circumstances, the frowns or the favors of fortune.

Index

INDEX

Index

The Lakeside Classics